Freedom with Order

The Doctrine of the Church
in the United Church of Christ

Robert S. Paul

United Church Press
New York

The biblical quotations in this book are, unless otherwise indicated, from
the *Revised Standard Version of the Bible,* copyright 1946, 1952, and ©
1971, 1973 by the Division of Christian Education, National Council of
Churches, and are used by permission. Quotations marked NEB are from
The New English Bible. © The Delegates of the Oxford University Press
and the Syndics of the Cambridge University Press, 1961. The excerpt
marked PHILLIPS is from the Revised edition of *The New Testament in
Modern English* by J.B. Phillips and is reprinted with permission of
Macmillan Publishing Company, Inc. © J.B. Phillips 1958, 1960, 1972. The
quotation marked KJV is from the King James Version.

Library of Congress Cataloging-in-Publication Data

Paul, Robert S.
   Freedom with order.

   Bibliography: p. 137.
   1. Church—History of doctrines.   2. United Church
of Christ—Doctrines.   I.
Title.
BV598.P39   1987   262   87-4992
ISBN 0-8298-0749-7 (pbk.)

United Church Press, 132 West 31 Street, New York, NY 10001

Contents

Foreword by Avery D. Post   v

Preface   vii

Introduction   ix

Chapter 1: The Doctrine of the Church   1
     What Is Ecclesiology?   1
     The Paradox of the Church   3
     Sources   4
     A Theology of the Church   6
     The Quest for Authority   7

Chapter 2: Our Inherited Ecclesiologies (I)   9
     Evangelical Traditions   9
         The *Evangelische* Tradition   10
         The "Christian" Tradition   14

Chapter 3: Our Inherited Ecclesiologies (II)   16
     Reformed Ecclesiologies   16
         Calvin and the Church   19
     Reformed Confessions   27
     Congregational Ecclesiology   33

Chapter 4: Assessment of Traditional
         Ecclesiologies   40
     How Far Are Our Traditional
         Ecclesiologies Still Valid?   41
     The Lessons of New Testament
         Restorationism   46

Ecclesiology and the Need for Basic
        Authority   49

Chapter 5: The Old and the New   51
        The UCC Constitution and Bylaws   53

Chapter 6: The Doctrine of the Church (I)   60

Chapter 7: The Doctrine of the Church (II)   73

Chapter 8: The Doctrine of the Church (III)   82

Chapter 9: The Place of Pragmatism   89

Chapter 10: The Doctrine of the Church (IV):
        Two Ecclesiologies   100
    The Church in Mercersburg Theology   102
    The Doctrine of the Church in Peter
        Taylor Forsyth   113

Epilogue   124

Appendix: The Autonomy of the Local Church:
        Historical Perspective   127

Notes   137

Foreword

We can be grateful that theological literature is beginning to burgeon in the United Church of Christ. Our apparent theological dormancy has been of concern. An awakening has been expected for a decade or more. The fact that some of the new theological writing evidences a spirit of alarm over the destiny of our church in no way diminishes the value of the manifold contributions now being made in the search for a particular theological idiom.

We also can be happy that the scholars in the family are making valuable contributions to this serious effort. When the notable church historian Robert S. Paul, an ordained minister of the UCC now teaching at Austin Theological Seminary in Austin, Texas, presented theological addresses in the Pennsylvania Southeast Conference, the reverberations from those presentations were felt throughout the church. Indeed, there has been a broad eagerness to see his material in print. Now we have his book enabling us to savor his contributions and engage them critically.

There has been puzzlement, and even some dismay, that a church as theologically well endowed as the United Church of Christ should have deferred serious theological work, particularly in the area of ecclesiology. "The act of courageous ecumenism" that gave us the union promised that this new church in the United States would take the lead and set the pace in developing "a timely ecumenical ecclesiology."

This aspect of the vocation of the United Church of Christ has developed too slowly. Nourishing us all along have been the "constituent ecclesiologies" in the traditions of the Evangelical and Reformed Church and the Congregational Christian Churches. In addition, as Dr. Paul observes, the preamble to the Constitution of the UCC reflects a significant and faithful theology of the church. Clearly there has been a promising basis for the growth of a strong and self-conscious doctrine of the Church in the United Church of

Christ. But we have not been working on ecclesiology in a disciplined way and so find ourselves, as I have elsewhere expressed it, in a condition of ecclesiological deficit.

Given these realities, it is not surprising that Dr. Paul, out of his considerable fervor and scholarship, has filed in sections of this book a bill of complaints against those forces in the church that have kept it from ecclesiological maturity. Those sections should energize the critical response to the book. Some will agree; many will disagree. Those who think that they have found reinforcement for their prejudices should look deeper for the essential affirmation of UCC history that runs all the way through Professor Paul's book.

To say that the United Church of Christ is obsessed with polity would be extreme, but there has been an uncommon degree of polity self-consciousness resulting in the development of the church's Constitution and Bylaws. Readers of *Freedom with Order* will welcome the firm statement that polity is always secondary to ecclesiology and, further, that ecclesiology is governed by Christology.

What may be most valuable in these chapters is the kind, quality, and depth of resource that a church historian brings to a high and catholic view of the church. The *jure divino* view of the church is articulated carefully. The "gift of Pentecost" is given great emphasis, resulting in the claim that "ecclesiology is essentially pneumatology." The church is seen as "a necessary part of the gospel," with its reality strongly exhibited in acts of covenant and mutual ministry. All this orthodoxy concerning the nature of the church is seen with particular reference to the UCC's theological parentage in Luther, Calvin, Zwingli, Robert Browne, and the Mercersburg teachers. The perspectives of P.T. Forsyth, one of Dr. Paul's theological parents, are in evidence throughout the book.

If this book makes a distinctive contribution in the search of United Church of Christ people for a "truly ecumenical theology," it may be in the way in which the tension between freedom and order is described. While respecting the history of church order, Dr. Paul is wary of absolute forms of ecclesiastical order. He makes the case for "flexibility in church structures" and counsels an evangelical pragmatism in church life, based confidently in the freedom and power of the Holy Spirit, indeed a practicality that both roots in and serves the gospel.

Avery D. Post
President
United Church of Christ

Preface

Since World War II there has been a growing conviction that we cannot legitimately separate doctrine from ethics: there is an indivisible relationship between what Christians profess in matters of faith and how they act in society.

But the time has now come when we should also recognize that doctrine and ethics must include ecclesiology. That is, there is also an inescapable relationship between the way churches are organized and governed, the gospel they proclaim, and the ethics they demonstrate: how essentially *Christian* is the government expressed by papacy, episcopacy, presbyterianism, or congregationalism?

Consideration of our own doctrine of the church in the United Church of Christ as an ecumenical experiment in ecclesiology should also convince us that such questions can no longer adequately be dealt with denominationally, separate from the total ecumenical context in which our church finds itself. Indeed, the appearance of *Baptism, Eucharist, and Ministry* and *The COCU Consensus: In Quest of a Church of Christ Uniting* provide indications that the ecumenical context of ecclesiology is now increasingly recognized.

It is with these convictions that this book has been penned. For the rest, it is perhaps sufficient to say that it is offered as a theological commentary to be read alongside Louis H. Gunnemann's excellent historical survey *The Shaping of the United Church of Christ* (1977).

The material for this book was first offered to ministers in a convocation on theology organized by the Pennsylvania Southeast Conference in 1980. My thanks are due to John Shetler, who was then Minister of that particular Conference and to all those associated with him for the hospitality we enjoyed at Mensch Mill on that occasion. My thanks also go to the participants whose contributions have been incorporated into my revision of the lectures.

For the rest, my thanks are due to those United Church of Christ students who have found their way, through the years, into the Presbyterian seminaries in which I have served and who, by their questions, have helped define both the content and the form of this book; and to my wife, Eunice, for helping me, more than she can realize, to put the manuscript into printable form.

Introduction

The first part of any book must introduce the reader to the major concern that has to be treated, and this book is no exception. Harry Rudin is reputed to have made the somewhat cynical remark that if an organization carries the word United in its title, that is a fairly clear indication that it is not. There appears to be more than a grain of truth in that, for organizations like the United Nations, the former United Arab Republic, and even the United Steelworkers have not been noticeable for demonstrations of unity. Indeed our very concern for the nature of the church has arisen at least in part because our denomination brought together Christians of several traditions on the basis of their common allegiance to Jesus Christ without applying itself immediately to the necessary task of working out the implications of that common faith for what we believed about the church, its worship, organization, and ministry.

The thoughts of this book can be put into clearer perspective if they are seen as part of the unfinished business from the union that brought the UCC into being. I think we might observe, against the caustic comment quoted above, that the word United in our title was not intended to describe an actuality, but a purpose, an intention, an ultimate goal. We know we are imperfect, and we recognize that in many ways we remain disunited, but our *intention* is to move toward the time when unity in the church will be an actuality.

However, if this intention is to be anything but a pious dream, the time has come—indeed I would argue that it is overdue—when we should examine how the common faith we proclaim affects the very nature and shape of the religious community into which we believe we have been called. How should this common faith affect the way in which we worship, the way in which we organize ourselves and administer our ecclesiastical institutions, or how does it influence the way in which we express our mission to the world and our ministry to one another? We are not simply a band of devout people who casually congregate Sunday by Sunday to express pious ideas about God or political ideas about society, as others might choose to congregate to play golf or watch football. There is an imperative involved in our gathering together, and we should be clear about the Source of that imperative, and about its implications, not only for what we say in Christ's name about our society, but also for the kind of community we claim to be. That is ecclesiology, the doctrine of the church.

It cannot be ignored because the kind of fellowship we are (or become) is an integral part of the gospel we proclaim. A church cannot effectively proclaim God's love and concern for society if its own institutional structure is a practical denial of that gospel. Robert McAfee Brown cited a medieval manuscript that described the church as something like Noah's ark: if it were not for the storm outside, you could not stand the stench inside.[1] He also noted Reinhold Niebuhr's comment that if the church is to survive, it will have to survive despite the storm and the stench. That represents the very nature of the paradox in any doctrine of the church, to which we will have to return: the church does survive despite threats from without and within. Although we cannot do much about the storms without, we can do something about the stench within. This is the point at which our ecclesiology becomes not only important, but also imperative.

It is an imperative because the church itself is an integral part of its own gospel. There is little use in proclaiming a gospel of reconciliation to the world if the church reveals, by the way it runs its own affairs, that it is unreconciled. This is why ecumenical commitment within the UCC must never be allowed to slip into a secondary place within our own purpose as a church (denomination).

The UCC has a unique ecumenical contribution arising from its own history. Not only does it draw from both the "magisterial" and the "radical" Reformations (through the Schwenkfelder Church), but the church constituency contains all three of the major polities. If the German Reformed tradition represents presbyterial (consistorial) church government, and the Congregational Christian Churches express congregationalism, through the Hungarian Reformed churches (Calvin Synod) we include a form of episcopacy, although it is of the New Testament and practical kind rather than the prelatical form often to be found elsewhere.

However, historical circumstances alone do not constitute sufficient reason for the ecumenical imperative. We have to remind those who frame our policies that our church claims an ecumenical goal not because this is a good idea, or because Christian unity makes sound common sense within a depressed economy, or because we feel indifferent to differences of doctrine and worship, but solely because Christ calls us to it; and to proclaim reconciliation to the rest of society, while the churches themselves remain unreconciled to one another, is hypocritical and basically a denial of the gospel entrusted to us. Our allegiance is to Jesus Christ and the mission entrusted to the whole church—ecclesiology is, in that sense, secondary, for our allegiance is not primarily to it—but because the way in which a church worships, organizes itself, and engages in mission is itself primary evidence of the good news we proclaim, it is itself a primary concern of our mission.

We have to get our priorities straight. My concern for ecclesiology in this book is not because we are committed to one or more views of the church that have been handed down to us, important though such historic traditions may be, but because our primary commitment is to Jesus Christ and to the gospel that centers in God's act of grace to us men and women in Bethlehem, Calvary, and the Empty Tomb. It is as the community of those whose unity centers in that gospel that the doctrine of the church is important, because a church proclaims that Good News, not only in what is declared from its pulpits, but also by *what it is*.

Chapter 1
The Doctrine of the Church

WHAT IS ECCLESIOLOGY?

The term ecclesiology needs definition. Historically it has been used for two kinds of ecclesiastical studies. When it first appeared in the nineteenth century it was applied particularly to church architecture, so that it might truly be said that the original application of the word was "simple antiquarianism."[1] Obviously I am using the term in the much broader sense of the study of the church not as a building, but as an institution, not in terms of physical structure and decoration in ecclesiastical architecture, but in terms of its essential form as a divine and human society. It is the church's doctrine of itself as it is related to the gospel.

Here we may profitably remind ourselves of the basic meaning behind the word ėkklēsía from which the English words ecclesiology, ecclesiastical, and their derivatives have sprung. It essentially means "those who are called out," "an assembly," from ʾékklētos (called out) and the verb ėkkalēīn (to call out). There has been a strong Protestant emphasis on the implications of this calling out, and there have been those in our history who have stressed it in terms of the church's call to holiness, and that aspect of the church's calling cannot be entirely discounted: there is a legitimate sense in which the People of God, from the time of Abraham onward, was called by God to be a people separated from the rest of the world to be a holy people.

But sometimes this emphasis on the church's separation to holiness has taken precedence over the equally important fact that if the church is called out to be a special people, it is called out *by God:* it is God who does the calling, whose call guarantees its holiness and

1

gives it its special vocation. The distinction between the church and the world is important only as we recognize that the call comes from God. The church is *not* a voluntary society in the sense that we choose to belong to it, like deciding to become a Rotarian or joining a health spa. We may indeed decide to link ourselves with a particular church, but the church *itself* is called into being by God, and truly to belong to the Great Church is to be called into it by God. Even Robert Browne, who has been regarded as the father of Separatism, saw that. Here is his definition of the church:

> The Church planted or gathered, is a company or number of Christians or believers, which by a willing covenant made with their God, are under the government of God and Christ, and keep his laws in one holy communion: because Christ hath redeemed them unto holiness and happiness for ever, from which they were fallen by the sin of Adam.[2]

There is no doubt about where the initiative lies in this. It is God's action that brings the church into being, and the center of the church covenant is first of all with God and only secondarily with one another. It has been the erosion of the doctrine of the church during the past 100 or 150 years that has tended to invert that order and to concentrate on the purely human and societal aspects of the church.

In God's sight the church is certainly distinct from the world, separate and holy to God and the divine purposes, but we must concentrate on the fact that *God* does the calling and recognize that the church's holiness does not belong to itself except as it is related to Jesus Christ. The church is perhaps closest to its essential "called-outness" when it gathers to worship God.

I am suggesting that ecclesiology is the teaching or doctrine about the church essentially and most distinctively as a society of those who are called out by God, first of all in assembling together in worship, then in regulating their affairs before the world, and then again in conducting mission and ministry. The church has to be concerned that its conduct, or that of its members, does not become a scandal against the gospel it preaches, but let the question of its *holiness*—the assessment of the moral purity of its members, which obsessed some of our forebears sometimes even to the point of spiritual arrogance—be left to the judgment of God alone: it is sufficient for us that God has called us *as a community* to be the kind of community in which Christ's realm is centered.

THE PARADOX OF THE CHURCH

The church is obviously a human society. If it were not, it would not be bothered by the storms without and there would be no "stench within." We must acknowledge this essentially human character of the church because it has been persistently downplayed by every "high church" position—from high church Catholicism, through the "high church" positions taken by some of those within our own Reformed tradition, to the "high church" Separatist positions. And whenever that happens there is the danger of virtually deifying the church—the sin of ecclesiolatry.

At the same time there *is* a divine element in the constitution of the church that creates a paradox. The temptation of every humanist or pragmatic approach to the church is to ignore this and treat the church as if it were *merely* a human institution; if that were so, we have no "good news" for human society. That is the temptation of every rationalist or "low church" approach to churchmanship. To deny the divine nature of the church's call and the divine imperative of its mission is ultimately to abdicate the gospel and reduce the church to the character of a country club, or (a little better) a service club or political pressure group.

By the very nature of its call and its mission the church is a paradox. Every perceptive writer on the subject in recent years has had to recognize this characteristic as fundamental to any constructive understanding of the church. Claude Welch's *The Reality of the Church* was described as an attempt "to view the church in the wholeness of its being, as an historical community of human beings existing in response to the creative and redemptive work of God."[3] Robert McAfee Brown, in the opening chapter of *The Significance of the Church,*[4] entitled "A Long Hard Look at the Church," examined that paradox in a series of trenchant criticisms of the kind that we recognize as all too familiar, and often all too true. The paradox is reflected in such titles as *The Misunderstanding of the Church,* by Emil Brunner,[5] and *The Strangeness of the Church,* by Daniel Jenkins.[6]

But the feature of the church that makes for this "misunderstanding" in the world, this "strangeness," is the essential relationship between its very human character and its divine call. If the church could be considered only in terms of the former or the latter, there

3

would be no paradox. It is the divine call and mission to a human society that gives it its "reality" and significance. That is the characteristic that forces the church to wrestle with a "doctrine" about itself. And that is something that in these pragmatic days we have been in danger of forgetting. Our temptation has been precisely the opposite one to the temptation of earlier writers: they concentrated on its divine call so that they were often in danger of deifying the church; our temptation has been so to concentrate on the church's obviously human character, the ways in which it may be subjected to sociological, psychological, and historical analysis, that we ignore the divine call and mission. When that happens we are in danger of losing the gospel itself, and without a gospel there is not only no justification for any "church," but also little reason for claiming to be Christian. The paradox of the church's essential nature is basic to all that I shall consider in this work. Because of it, and because it is carried within its communal character, the gospel proclaims that, in the sight of God, the redemption and reconciliation offered to us in Jesus Christ is related not only to individuals, but to human society as well.

SOURCES

But one cannot assert the *divine* side of this ecclesiastical paradox without being prepared to say on what authority that assertion can be made. The church does not have a divine call simply because Christians claim it—at least, if that is the only reason we can give for that claim, then we must expect the world to remain unconvinced. There is no *earthly* reason why anyone should take the church's claims seriously, unless we can either produce independent testimony or provide a good reason why our own testimony should be taken with special seriousness. The testimony of the church itself *is* important, and perhaps in the final analysis it provides hard evidence for its claims in the modern world, but it will not mean much unless, side by side with its *claim* to a miraculous birth and survival in history, and its testimony to a worldwide mission, there is also evidence that in a realistic, if figurative, sense it is the Body of Christ, and that it does in fact give evidence of the fruits of the Spirit: "love, joy, peace, patience, kindness, goodness, fidelity, gentleness, and self-control [Gal. 5:21]." Obviously crusades, inquisitions and persecutions do not help that testimony; but neither do the things

4

that accompany competitive denominationalism, or our indifference to the world's need, or our practical unbelief in the very things we are supposed to be proclaiming.

One of the basic insights of the Puritans was that doctrine must never be divorced from ethics. It is no use proclaiming God's universal love if we do not live it in relation to others, especially to other Christians; it is little use proclaiming that our gospel centers in resurrection if we are giving a lifelong illustration of the maxim to "eat, drink and be merry, for tomorrow we die"; it is no use preaching reconciliation if we have not yet been reconciled ourselves, even to others who profess the name of Jesus Christ. Ecclesiology is part of *practical* Christianity: this community has to *show* itself as the living, working Body of Christ, not only in what it does vis-à-vis the world, but also in the way it organizes itself, in its shape, its life-style and worship.

I will have to return to this theme, but for the moment I will look at the source of the church's basic claim to be the community called into being by God.

Obviously the church is not the church of Jesus Christ just because it says it is, but because *God* says it is. It is vitally important to get this clear because the Reformation took place on that very issue. If there is any doubt about the church's claims about itself, then it must be able to bring independent testimony not of its own word, but of God's Word. Hence the Reformers' emphasis on the scriptures as the Word of God, a crucially important corrective to the claims of the church of that time about itself.

But there is no need to remind you that the time soon came when the Bible was asserted in the same exclusive, infallible, and deified way as the papal decrees of the past, and alongside the ecclesiolatry—the worship of itself—practiced by historic churches of both East and West there was a new error, bibliolatry—the worship of the literal word of scripture. So we are faced with the basic problem of authority in all our consideration of the church today—on what basis, by what authority does the church claim to be the church of Jesus Christ, and to what authority can it appeal to define and regulate its structure, administration, and worship? If we are to have a gospel—good news—for the modern world, we cannot indefinitely postpone the consideration of that problem, and yet it is a problem that the churches have persistently refused to address seriously since the biblical theology of the 1950s became discredited by J.A.T. Robinson's *Honest to God,*[7] and by all that has followed since.

Before I can go much further in defining the nature of the church, or resolve the problems of ecclesiology, I must address the problem of our underlying authority for claiming to be what we claim to be, and it is clear that the answer cannot be as simplistic as either it was assumed to be in the development of Catholicism, or as it was assumed to be in the Protestant restatements.

A THEOLOGY OF THE CHURCH

Before I proceed one point must be made: there is no absolute but God. The constant temptation of humanity is to find an image that is more proximate to us, and to worship that in the place of God. The church and its ministry, the Bible, Christian experience, and even human rationality are all testimonies to the will of God, *but they are only testimonies:* they are not to be worshiped in the place of God. The church's development in history *is* an important testimony for the church because Jesus Christ *did* confer the gift of the Holy Spirit, and because the church *was* given authority in certain areas of Christian life, but when this authority was made an absolute, it became a denial of the very thing that it was claiming. So, too, the scriptures are a vitally important testimony that enabled our forebears to correct the idolatrous pretensions of the church of their time—it *is* the primary expression of God's Word—but it also remains human, and carries within it the errors of fact and comprehension that are common to humanity. I might comment on other testimonies to God's Spirit in the church: the answer to the problem of Authority is not as simple as we have usually wanted to make it.

Fundamentally we are concerned with God. The secondary testimonies are important only as they point to God and not to themselves. The Fourth Evangelist recorded a statement about the essential character of the Holy Spirit's testimony that is vitally important at this point: Jesus said, "But when the Spirit of truth comes he will lead you to the complete truth, *since he will not be speaking from himself* but will say only what he has learnt. . . . He will glorify me, since all he tells you will be taken from what is mine [John 16:13–15, PHILLIPS]." Theology, indeed *Christ*ology, governs ecclesiology: *the church points to God through Jesus Christ.*

This should be another basic axiom for our study, and it is obviously related to the paradox of the church that was cited earlier.

We are faced with the principle of the Incarnation. The Catholic branches of the church and the Mercersburg theologians were right in claiming that. Where such catholic movements, however, have tended to go astray is in claiming too much from that doctrine. The Holy Spirit *has* led the church, but God's will is not to be identified with *our understanding* of where that Spirit has been leading us. Our understanding of "the truth" must not be granted the same infallibility (i.e., "authority") that belongs to the living Christ. The church must never, for example, claim that Christ's own sinlessness is transferred to the church itself. This leads directly to the sin of ecclesiolatry.

But with that qualification, to be discussed later, let us accept the principle that since the church points the world to God in Christ, the doctrine of the church—ecclesiology—must be basically concerned with theology, and even Christology: and at the center of that there is the Incarnation.

Those who come from the Evangelical and Reformed tradition within the United Church of Christ may be particularly interested in Luther J. Binkley's words: "If the central doctrine of the Mercersburg Theology was Christology, then the most important corollary of this view was the doctrine of the Church."[8] There were dangers in this, as there are in any catholicizing movement, but there is also a fundamental truth: our ecclesiology must point to the Incarnation of Jesus Christ, or it will compromise its essential testimony. Our doctrine of the church is not to be assumed solely from the church's historical development, nor to be extrapolated literally from the way the church organized itself in the time of the New Testament. Rather, it is to point *to a communal expression of what God revealed to us about the divine nature in Jesus Christ.*

THE QUEST FOR AUTHORITY

What appears under this subject has been dealt with, to some extent, in chapter 6 of *Ministry*[9] and, in a more extended form, in chapter 2 of *The Church in Search of Its Self.*[10] In the latter work I pointed out that in a strange but convincing way, the various channels of spiritual authority, by which the churches seek to authenticate their own claims, run curiously parallel to Ernst Troeltsch's three types of the church.[11] The three basic channels of authority that have been manifested in church history are (1) the church itself, its hierarchy and tradition; (2) the Bible; and (3) the immediate guidance of the Holy Spirit in individual experience.

Each of these has to be recognized as an authentic channel of grace, but the problem arises when churches appeal to any one of them exclusively, without recognizing the authentic claims of the others. Furthermore, there is a particular problem with regard to the last of these, in which the nontheological means of reaching spiritual truth—human "reason"—can too easily be confused with the immediate revelation of the Holy Spirit in individual experience.

It may be providential that all churches are now having to review their traditional (and exclusive) understandings of the Authority issue, and this opens the possibility that they may be encouraged to look at the question ecumenically.

The importance of the issue for our contemporary churches is seen not only in the difficulty that ecclesiastical leaders often have in gaining the support of the rank and file for many of their social policies, but also in the problem of identity that has afflicted many denominations, including our own, since World War II. I have tried to keep the issue in the spotlight, but it really demands a full-length treatment.[12]

Chapter 2
Our Inherited
Ecclesiologies (I)

EVANGELICAL TRADITIONS

Let us now look at the four distinct ecclesiological traditions that have been inherited in the United Church of Christ. From the Evangelical and Reformed Church we have two traditions that arose directly from the Reformation: the *evangelische* tradition, which goes directly back to the ecclesiology of Martin Luther, and the Reformed tradition, which may be traced through Ursinus, Olevianus, and the Heidelberg Catechism to John Calvin. Through the Congregational Christian Churches we have the Reformed tradition as it was developed and modified by the Congregational Puritans, and the evangelical tradition of the "Christian" movement that was born on the American frontier.

Before looking at these traditions in more detail two points are to be noted:

1 Within the earlier churches that united to form the UCC there was a strong "Reformed" element and an equally strong constituency that preferred the word Evangelical to describe itself. Without building too much on that, since those same words—Evangelical and Reformed—can be maintained in very different ways, it could be significant for our purpose. It suggests that, on both sides of our major denominational constituency, there was a sense in which we held ourselves to be basically Reformed in respect to our essential doctrine, but as modified by the Evangelical experience rediscovered by Luther, and as it had been interpreted in the context of the New World.

2. I have used the word ecclesiology and not "polity." I am basically concerned not with polity, whether congregational or presbyterian, but with *the way in which the church understands itself*

and its relation to the gospel. The question of polity is secondary, and ultimately irrelevant, except as it may become an expression of the gospel. In some ways the founders of the UCC may be criticized for having been lax in leaving those matters to be decided later; but in another sense we have to thank God that they did because that itself was a tacit recognition that all questions of government are dependent on the nature of the church and its mission. The matter of polity is not to be imposed on any church, but is to evolve out of the life, witness, and mission of the church, a necessary expression of the very gospel it proclaims.

Both the congregational and the presbyterian forms of polity are known and revered in certain parts of our church family, and we have nothing to be ashamed of in acknowledging that. But the formation of the UCC (with all its faults) made possible the relegation of the polity question to its proper place; it is to be the servant and expression of church life and witness, *not the precondition for its pattern.* We start from the premise that what the church has to proclaim and how it proclaims it will determine the way it is governed and not vice versa. This is a genuine recapturing of the spirit of the New Testament, for which we should be profoundly grateful. Given our inherited prejudices, on both sides, about polity, we could have spent the best part of eternity arguing that point while the UCC waited in the wings to be born.

Let us look first at the Evangelical traditions inherited by the UCC because they represent something in Christianity that is older than the Reformed traditions. Only when the evangelical mission and ministry of the church goes sour does it need to be reformed. Whether we start with the New Testament or with Luther's reaffirmation of the evangelical faith in the sixteenth century, the proclamation of the evangel is central.

The Evangelische Tradition

Luther's doctrine of the Church started with the rediscovery of Justification by Faith. We became Christian (and hence a Christian community) by our acknowledgment that we are justified in the eyes of God not by what we have done, not by our acceptance of a sacramental system, not by being born into a certain christianized culture, but by faith in what God has done for us in Jesus Christ. The other things may be helpful, and even important, but faith in what God has done is central. *God's grace is central: sola gratia.*

Once that is given its priority, it is bound radically to affect the doctrine of the church itself. If faith is put at the center, then it leads directly to a doctrine of the Priesthood of All Believers because the heart of Christian churchmanship is not in the things that can be done for us only by a special order of clergy, but through a ministry in which all God's people have their proper part to play and that is exercised mutually on behalf of one another.

In the same way, the authority of the Bible becomes central to the Reformers, not because they consciously started with scripture in a desire to undercut the historical development of the church or undermine the papacy, but because they rediscovered justification by faith at the center of the biblical record. The principle of *sola scriptura* may have been an inevitable consequence of that, and the reform of the church according to the biblical testimony essentially a consequence of that insight into the nature of faith in New Testament times. It certainly recognized that priority regarding the faith had to be given to the historic record.

However, once that priority had been granted, there was always the temptation to take the *details* of ecclesiastical order in the New Testament and put them at the center of church reform. There was always a struggle between the evangelical principle of justification by faith and biblical literalism, which we see reflected even in our own day. The movement of Luther's own thought on the church illustrates this struggle.

Luther's 1520 treatise *On the Papacy at Rome* has been described as "the earliest of his writings to present a full outline of his teachings on the nature of the Christian Church,"[1] and in that work the evangelical principle clearly predominates. He defined the church as "all who live in true faith, hope and love; so that the essence of the church is not a bodily assembly, but an assembly of hearts in one faith, as St. Paul says, 'one baptism, one faith, one Lord.'"[2] As I have pointed out elsewhere, Luther is not too concerned about the *visible* marks of the church at that point, but with its spiritual reality, because that was the vital aspect of the church that he felt had been lost.[3] That was the aspect of New Testament Christianity that had to be recaptured.

At the same time Luther did not discount the visible marks of the church. In the same treatise he said: "The external marks, whereby one can perceive where the Church is on earth, are baptism, the

Sacrament, and the Gospel; and not Rome, or this place, or that."[4] This immediately raises the question, Who had the right to administer baptism and the Lord's Supper, or to define the authentic faith that constituted the gospel? How was the individual to distinguish between sacraments and faith that were authentic and those that were spurious? Sooner or later Luther himself would be forced to come to grips with the church as a visible, organized entity; but for the moment his main concern was to reaffirm the spiritual dimension of *faith* that he had discovered at the heart of the New Testament community.

Luther illustrates the tension between the evangelical principle and a literal appeal to the New Testament in what I regard as the second stage in developing his own ecclesiology. There is evidence that during the years 1523–25 he moved clearly in a "Restorationist" direction, both in the instructions he sent out to the parish at Leisnig and in his letter to the Bohemian Brethren who had written for his advice. The Bohemians had been in the habit of gaining ordination for their bishops by the subterfuge of bribery or intrigue with renegade Italian bishops. Luther argued that this was unnecessary, and that the Bohemians could simply follow the apostolic practice. He argued that at the time of Paul, "the authority and dignity of priesthood resided in the community of believers," and that the Christian rights of this community of believers

> demand that one, or as many as the community chooses, shall be chosen or approved who, in the name of all with these rights, shall perform these functions publicly, otherwise there might be shameful confusion among the people of God, and a kind of Babylon in the Church, where everything should be done in order, as the Apostle teaches [I Corinthians 14:40]. For it is one thing to exercise a right publicly; another to use it in time of emergency. Publicly one may not exercise a right without consent of the whole body of the Church. In time of emergency each may use it as he deems best.[5]

He suggested that Christians who wanted a more reformed church should assemble themselves for prayer to petition "our Lord for his help," and that they should then, in full confidence,

> bring your supplications and prayers that he may send his Spirit into your hearts. For he works in you, or rather, works in you both to will and to do [Philippians 2:13]. For if this thing is to be done

auspiciously and to continue successfully, it is necessary that there be in you the divine strength which, as Peter testifies, God supplies [I Peter 4:11].[6]

The thing we must notice about Luther's ecclesiology, even in his recourse to the New Testament apostolic pattern of the church, is that he never presented the apostolic practice in a literalistic or legalistic way. The New Testament practice was likely to be the best way for the church because the apostles are our authority, and they provide us with the best starting point for the way in which the church should be organized, but Luther's appeal to scripture was always balanced by his determination to maintain the spiritual, the *faith* basis of New Testament ecclesiology, and by the practical situation of the church in his own day. This was a valuable modification of the Restorationist principle. Luther is a prime example of "evangelical pragmatism" in ecclesiological matters—that is, one who believed that pragmatic considerations should control the form and organization of the church—not for purely practical reasons, but to enable the church to fulfill its own divinely given ministry and mission.

We can see something of this evangelical spirit in Luther in the passage that immediately follows the suggestion that a congregation should come together in prayer and then act in full confidence that the Holy Spirit would bless their efforts.

> Then call or come together freely, as many as have been touched in heart by God to think and judge as you do. Proceed in the name of the Lord to elect one or more whom you desire, and who appear worthy and able. Then let those who are leaders among you lay hands upon them, and certify and commend them to the people and the church or community. In this way let them become your bishops, ministers, or pastors. Amen. The qualifications of those to be elected are fully described by Paul in Tit. 1[:6ff.], and I Tim. 3[:2ff.].[7]

Luther took the pattern of the church in the New Testament seriously and regarded it as the normal starting point for all ecclesiology.

But I disagree here with those Lutheran writers for whom the Letter to the Bohemians may be something of an embarrassment, since it pointed in a direction that was to be taken by the Anabaptists. Conrad Bergensdoff, for example, argues that the Letter to the

Bohemians outlines simply Luther's suggestions for an emergency situation.[8] I do not think that can be sustained by the evidence itself, for Luther clearly thought that in an emergency, any baptized Christians could fulfill the functions of the priesthood; here he was clearly suggesting that the *normal* starting place for church organization and practice should be sought in the apostolic example.[9]

But although Luther took the pattern of New Testament churchmanship seriously, he did not suggest that it had to be followed slavishly. The Holy Spirit *could* lead the church into new ways. Later, political considerations would cause him to radically modify his recommendations in ecclesiology and depend extensively on the authority of civil rulers. What we must notice about Luther's ecclesiology is not so much the details of the way in which Lutheran churches organized themselves in Europe, or later in America, but the way in which Luther, while starting from the biblical pattern, was ready to modify it in terms of what the Spirit was saying to the churches in his own day.

The "Christian" Tradition

The other part of the Evangelical legacy in the UCC comes from the "Christian" churches of the American frontier.

In one sense it was simply an Anglo-Saxon version of the evangelical experience that we find in Luther. Justification by Faith, the Priesthood of All Believers, and the principle of *sola scriptura* were objectified on the American frontier in the conversion experience, in the democratic practices of local churches, and in the simple biblical faith that was preached in conventicle and camp meeting. In some ways the tradition has all the immediacy, the directness, and sometimes the brashness of American culture in contrast to European; but it is a reminder to us that, much as we may deplore the excesses of American frontier religion, this continent was largely subdued and civilized because of it.

Perhaps the pattern closest to the Christian tradition that was absorbed earlier into the Congregational Christian Churches is that of the Christian Church (Disciples), with whom we have been trying to enter into a closer relationship. When we look at the ecclesiological patterns adopted by that tradition on the frontier, we find that all the evangelical constituents in Luther were also present there, although some of the emphases may have been different: both appeal to the New Testament pattern, and evangelical pragmatism was very much in evidence, as was the evangelical commitment to Justification by Faith.

But the mixture is different, and the result has an unmistakably American accent. The appeal to the simple letter of the scriptures is so strong (in opposition to the false complexities that the frontier preachers believed had been introduced by church theologians) that it produced an inevitable tension between their restorationism, which tried to restore the exact pattern of New Testament Christianity, and their ecumenical insistence that all Christians should be one. This remains a tension among Evangelicals to this day—the problem that restorationism that starts with the New Testament pattern can become a new form of ecclesiastical legalism, and that insistence on Christian unity, *which ought to be inclusive,* can, because of that tension, become exclusive.

There we see the dangers, but we like to think that the original insistence of the frontier "Christians" on the oneness of all Christian believers, and recognition that the human element can poison Christian relationships in the name of orthodoxy, have been incorporated into the UCC's continuing ecumenical commitment and in its insistence that creeds and convenants need constantly to be measured by the eternal gospel. We cannot yet claim the distinction claimed by the "Christians" of the frontier, that we are simply "Christians," but we are working on it.

In some ways the "Christian" tradition incorporated into the earlier Congregational Christian Churches has been more completely absorbed than any other, to such an extent that it is often difficult to trace its continuing presence. Perhaps that points to something essential to our churchmanship if our ecumenical mission is to be accomplished—the willingness to lose ourselves and our denominational idiosyncrasies to achieve the wider goal of Christian unity: not to give up things essential, but to be willing to sink our identity in the Spirit of our Lord.

Chapter 3
Our Inherited
Ecclesiologies (II)

REFORMED ECCLESIOLOGIES

The Reformed Tradition—or perhaps I should say the Reformed traditions—that has been incorporated into the United Church of Christ has tended to predominate in our separate histories. This is because, both in the heritage of the German Reformed Church, with its direct relationship to Calvin and Heidelberg, and in New England Congregationalism, with its heritage in English Calvinism and its Puritan expressions, the doctrine of the Church was central and was manifested in particular polities—presbyterial (or consistorial) in the first case and congregational in the second. It is as well to remember that both forms were essentially restorationist in the sense they both claimed to take their stand on what they regarded as the New Testament pattern of the church.

This restorationism becomes clear in "The Grand Debate" concerning presbytery and the congregational way that was hammered out in the Westminster Assembly, 1643–45, on which I have been working for a number of years.[1] The program of that assembly had been explicitly laid down in the Solemn League and Covenant, which brought the Scots to the support of the English Parliament during the English Civil War, and the reform of the Church of England was to be explicitly "according to the Word of God and the example of the best reformed churches."[2]

All the issues in the debates were thrashed out on the basis of establishing the precise New Testament pattern. The arguments were essentially exegetical—sometimes invoking methods of exegesis that few of us would now accept—but the objective was clear: to establish the New Testament pattern as the norm of church government and practice for all time. The major reason the two sides were not able finally to agree was that both claimed their own system as *jure divino*—by divine right.

I will cite a single example from each side.

The congregational claim had been laid down by Henry Jacob in 1604. At the beginning of his little work *Reasons taken out of God's Word and the best humane testimonies proving a necessitie of reforming our Churches in England,* he made four basic assertions about the Church:

1. It is necessarie to reforme the Churches of England, their ministries and ceremonies.
2. For the space of 200 years after Christ the Visible Churches using government were not Diocesan Churches, but particular ordinary Congregations only; and the Bishops (as they were peculiarly called after the Apostles) were only Parishionall and not Diocesan Bishops, differing from other Pastors only in prioritie of order not in majoritie of rule.
3. The Scriptures of the New Testament do containe & set forth unto us (besides the government of Extraordinary Officers, Apostles, Prophetes, Evangelists) an ordinary form of Church-government used then.
4. The ordinary form of Church-government set forth unto us in the New Testament, ought necessarily to be kept still by us; it is not changeable by men, and therefore it only is lawful.[3]

This is New Testament restorationism, and Jacob went on to ask, "Who is it that may presume to ordaine any forme of a Church save Christ only?"[4]

The presbyterian example may be taken from a book that the London Presbyterian ministers published in 1646 against the attempt of the English Parliament to establish a purely pragmatic form of presbyterian government in the church: *Jus Divinum Regiminis Ecclesiastici: or, the Divine Right of Church-Government, asserted and evidenced by the Holy Scriptures,* and the title page went on to claim "wherein it is proved that the Presbyterian Government, by Preaching and Ruling Elders, in Sessional, Presbyterial, and Synodical Assemblies, may lay the only claim to a Divine Right, according to the Holy Scriptures," This is New Testament restorationism, and it was made explicit when the authors laid out their thesis in the following logical steps:

The rule or standard of church government is only the holy Scriptures. Thus in the description, church government is styled a power or authority revealed in the holy Scriptures. For clearing hereof, take this proposition, viz.: Jesus Christ our Mediator hath laid down in his word a perfect and sufficient rule for the government of his visible Church under the New Testament, *which all the members of his Church ought to observe and submit unto until the end of the world.*[5]

This is restorationism, and both sides made precisely the same claims about their polities. The only point on which they disagreed was that one side read their Bibles and discovered a congregational system in the New Testament church, whereas the other side read the same Bible and insisted that the system was presbyterian.

The only issues for debate between the two groups were (a) what was the proper interpretation of worship, organization, and order in the church of the New Testament? and (b) what were the "best reformed churches"? The Presbyterians looked to the Reformed state churches on the continent of Europe and in Scotland, while the Congregationalists insisted that the churches of Jesus Christ had been even more reformed by the New England churches. And there were some, even on the continent of Europe, who thought that the congregational experiment was an improvement. Gisbert Voet, the distinguished Dutch preacher and theologian (sometimes described as the "pope of Utrecht") had described the exiled English Puritan churches as "the exact and perfect agreement of human actions with the law prescribed by God, accepted by real believers and followed with zeal."[6] This was high praise. At the beginning of the seventeenth century the issue between congregational and presbyterian polities among the Reformed churches had not yet hardened into fixed confessional attitudes as has happened since that time.

When the earliest documents are studied, another interesting feature of Reformed ecclesiology emerges. Although some Presbyterians of the English Civil War period, under the direct influence of the Scots commissioners to the Westminster Assembly, appear to have supported a *jure divino* basis for presbyterian polity, this was not true for the Reformed churches earlier. Both in the works of Calvin and in the Confessions there was certainly recognition that the church itself is of divine right, but *this assertion was not attached to any distinctive polity.* Indeed, on reading Calvin, one can see how both sides in the later Presbyterian/Congregational dispute could claim that they were being true to the Reformer.[7]

Calvin and the Church

Calvin's view of the church occurs in the first twelve chapters of Book IV of the *Institutes,* but a good deal of the material is taken up with attacking the position taken by the opposition—primarily the Roman Catholic Church, but also the Anabaptists and the Separatists, who, in the name of what they regarded as the essential purity of the church, separated from the *national* forms of the church. This *political* position of the Reformers needs to be borne in mind; they could establish only those forms of the church that would be sanctioned by the civil authorities, in Calvin's case the form that would be permitted by syndics of the civil oligarchy in Geneva.

When we separate Calvin's positive view of the church, demanded by the gospel, from his criticisms of the papacy and the sects, we find that his own ecclesiology is centered in Book IV, chapters i, iii, and xii and parts of chapters x (##27–32) and xi (##1–5). Nowhere is there any assertion that such a polity is *jure divino,* although clearly, by what happened in the city and state of Geneva, Calvin regarded the system of government as consistent with the gospel.

Perhaps it would be useful to consider just how far he did go in setting up a system of church government for the church, and what kind of order he felt was consistent with the gospel. However, he clearly thought that what he presented about the church in regard to government in the *Institutes* was all that was necessary because in laying out his subject matter for Book IV, he says: "Our plan of instruction now requires us to discuss the church, its government, orders, and power; then the sacraments, and lastly, the civil order."[8]

In passing, one should perhaps take note that this may indicate a different assumption from the one Calvin might take in our own day. He was speaking in a context in which, for more than 1,000 years, the church could assume that the civil ruler would be a Christian and would enforce the church's spiritual authority. How far would it be possible today to discuss civil society as a necessary extension of Christian faith and ecclesiastical authority?

Chapter 1 of Book IV of the *Institutes* deals with "The True Church with Which as Mother of All the Godly We must keep Unity." At once he asserted that the church and its ministry is instituted by God, and that the authority of the church is given to it directly by God.[9] There is the *jure divino* establishment of the church itself. The "Holy Catholic Church" of the creeds is both Visible and Invisible, and Calvin insisted that there was no good reason for the preposition in: it would be truer to say that we believe the Holy Catholic Church rather than to say that we believe *in* the church. This distinction is important because it declares that we do not put our trust in the church, *but in its testimony.*[10]

After a brief discussion of the Invisible Church and the Communion of Saints,[11] he turned to the Visible Church as the "mother" of all believers.[12] Here ministers and their teaching are to be acknowledged,[13] and membership comprises all the Elect of God[14]; but because God alone knows true faith, God "substituted for it a certain charitable judgment whereby we recognize as members of the church those who, by confession of faith, by example of life, and by partaking of the sacraments, profess the same God and Christ with us."[15] The marks of the church are clear and relatively simple:

> Wherever we see the Word of God purely preached and heard, and the sacraments administered according to Christ's institution, there, it is not to be doubted, a church of God exists. . . . For his promise cannot fail: "Wherever two or three are gathered together in my name, there I am in the midst of them." . . . If it [i.e., a church] has the ministry of the Word and honors it, if it has the administration of the sacraments, it deserves without doubt to be held and considered a church.[16]

Here we have the basis of a catholicity far wider than that practiced later by many Reformed churches, and Calvin went on to declare that if a church had these marks, however defective it might be in other respects, it was not to be denied.[17] Discipline as a distinctive feature of Reformed churchmanship, and even as a third mark of the church, may be implicit within Calvin, but it was never explicitly stated as such. Contrary to the way in which Calvin's churchmanship is often expounded, Calvin himself leaned toward generosity and inclusiveness, and he determinedly set his face against the rigor that leads to schism.[18]

Chapter ii is a comparison of the False and the True Church and is taken up with criticisms of the claims of the Roman papacy. In chapter iii Calvin returns to his own constructive ecclesiology in respect to the ministry of the Word.

After some preliminary sections in which he pointed to the need for ministry, the significance of ministry, and the prestige of the preaching office,[19] he looked at the biblical evidence in Ephesians for the distinctive forms of ministry in the church.[20] Like most of the Reformers, he distinguished between temporary officers established for the apostolic age alone—the apostles, prophets, and evangelists—and permanent officers—the pastors and teachers, "whom the church can never go without." But he does not exclude the possibility that if need arose, God could raise up the extraordinary apostolic offices again:

> Those who preside over the government of the church in accordance with Christ's institution are called by Paul as follows: first apostles, then prophets, thirdly evangelists, fourthly pastors, and finally teachers [Eph.4:11]. Of these only the last two have an ordinary office in the church; the Lord raised up the first three at the beginning of his Kingdom, and now and again revives them as the need of the times demands.[21]

Calvin was not as exclusively tied to the last two offices as later Reformed ecclesiology of all kinds became.[22] But he did maintain that the first three offices were not permanent in the church.

The church could never be without pastors and teachers. Teachers were not involved in discipline, the administration of sacraments, or pastoral oversight, but were concerned simply with maintaining the purity of doctrine; he thought that the pastoral office included all these functions within itself.[23] Just as teachers, in his view, corresponded to the prophets of the Old Testament, so also he believed that the pastors and bishops of the New Testament corresponded to the apostles in the early church.[24] A pastor was bound to his own church, although he could help in giving advice to other churches. Nevertheless, generally speaking, a pastor should not interfere in other churches. "This," he said, "is not of human devising but ordained by God."[25] To these two major forms of ministry—pastors and teachers—he also added deacons,[26] and restricted the ministry of women to helping the poor and the sick (the widows of 1 Timothy 5:9–10).

On the basis of the Pauline injunction that everything should be done "decently and in order [1 Cor. 14:40]," he said that "there is nothing in which order should be more diligently observed than in establishing government; for nowhere is there greater peril if anything be done irregularly."[27] Due attention should be paid both to the inner call that comes from God and to the "outer" call by which the church ratifies the call to ministry.[28] God calls the minister,[29] but the church has its part in ratifying this and the people also have their part:

We therefore hold that this call of a minister is lawful according to the Word of God, when those who seemed fit are created by the consent and approval of the people; moreover that other pastors ought to preside over the election in order that the multitude may not go wrong either through fickleness, through evil intentions, or through disorder.[30]

When such a person had been elected and the call ratified by the church, then the person should be ordained by the laying on of hands.

We can see from this that, in respect to the ministry, Calvin took the New Testament practice as his guide, that he did not argue for anything that he believed could not be explicitly proved from that practice. There was nothing in his ecclesiology at this point that all branches of the Reformed churches could not wholeheartedly endorse.

Most of Calvin's writings about the church in the first twelve chapters of Book IV of the *Institutes* are a survey of church history, with special reference to the way in which the church had been deflected from organizing itself in a manner consistent with its original gospel. But in the middle of chapter x he returned to his own constructive ecclesiology by commenting on the "Right ordering of church government and worship" and by laying down the principle that these matters should be governed by "decency, love and a free conscience."[31]

This is an extremely important practical principle. Calvin protested against those who argued against *all* order just because the ecclesiastical order practiced in the medieval church could be criticized. There is a necessity for church order, but notice the reason he gives for it.

First let us grasp this consideration. We see that some form of order is necessary in all human society to foster the common peace and maintain concord. We further see that in human transactions some procedure is always in effect, which is to be respected in the interests of public decency, and even of humanity itself. This ought especially to be observed in churches, which are best sustained when all things are under a well-ordered constitution, and which without concord become no churches at all.[32]

This principle of good order in both church and society, under the scriptures, was a most important element of Calvin's thought. He insisted on it in church government, but without extrapolating from scripture the details of what that church order should be. He developed this ecclesiology under two heads: "the first type pertains to rites and ceremonies; the second, to discipline and peace."[33] He insisted that where there was explicit dominical authority in respect to the church, it must be followed, but he did not extract from the scriptures, by inference, the kind of *jure divino* system of church government that his followers did on both sides of the polity issue. Here are his words:

> The Lord has in his sacred oracles faithfully embraced and clearly expressed both the whole sum of true righteousness, and all aspects of the worship of his majesty, and whatever was necessary to salvation; therefore, in these the Master alone is to be heard. But because he did not will in outward discipline and ceremonies to prescribe in detail what we ought to do (because he foresaw that this depended on the state of the times, and he did not deem one form suitable for all ages), here we must take refuge in those general rules which he has given, that whatever the necessity of the church will require for order and decorum should be tested against these. Lastly, because he has taught nothing specifically, and because these things are not necessary to salvation, and for the upbuilding of the church ought to be variously accommodated to the customs of each nation and age, it will be fitting (as the advantage of the church will require) to change and abrogate traditional practices and to establish new ones. Indeed, I admit that we ought not to charge into innovation rashly, suddenly, for insufficient cause. But love will best judge what may hurt or edify; and if we let love be our guide, all will be safe.[34]

Calvin had a much less doctrinaire position with regard to church order than many of those who later claimed to be strict Calvinists. He also insisted on a pragmatic principle that could well have been listened to by the Westminster divines: the prevention of error and abuse "will be attained if all observances, whatever they shall be, display manifest usefulness, and if very few are allowed."[35]

In chapters xi and xii he turned to ecclesiastical jurisdiction, and one would have expected him, here if nowhere else, to have set out the full panoply of church courts and ecclesiastical polity if he had regarded such a polity to be *jure divino*. But he did not. In chapter xi he entered into a detailed criticism of the way church discipline had been abused in the medieval papacy, and one of the basic emphases that comes through is his insistence that the only power proper to the church is *spiritual*. The basis for the ecclesiastical jurisdiction was in the power of the Keys (Matthew 18:15–18 and John 20:23), but he insisted that this power was to be set within the context of the preaching of the Word: "We conclude that in those passages the power of the keys is simply the preaching of the gospel, and that with regard to men it is not so much power as ministry. For Christ has not given this power actually to men, but to his Word, of which he has made men ministers."[36] This does not mean that Calvin ignored church discipline—quite the contrary—but how different this sounds from the punitive way in which ecclesiastical discipline was exercised in later Calvinism. The closest we come to it is in the words of John Cotton, when he asserted (following Calvin?) that power in the church was not an authority, but a ministry.

Calvin insisted that the only power proper to the church is spiritual.

> The holy bishops did not exercise their power through fines or prisons or other civil penalties but used the Lord's Word alone, as was fitting. For the severest punishment of the church, the final thunderbolt, so to speak, is excommunication, which is used only in necessity. Now this requires not physical force but is content with the power of God's Word.[37]

For this reason he held that ministers should have the right to call before them those who needed to be admonished privately or publicly.[38] But this right of disciplining did not rest in individual ministers, and he showed that, in the ancient church, the clergy always included the people in their deliberations. He cited Cyprian, who had said, "From the beginning of my episcopate I determined not to do anything without the advice of the clergy and the consent of the people."[39] Calvin added the comment—which may show some preference for collegial presbyterial order—that "the common and customary order was for the jurisdiction of the church to be exercised through the senate of elders."[40] The clear thrust of this passage, however, is that the people themselves have a vested interest in the way jurisdiction is administered, and that this is not to be exercised by individual ministers on their own authority. In other passages he seemed to incorporate not only the senate of elders in the acts of discipline, but also the vote of the believers.

> Now, that no one may despise such a judgment of the church or regard the condemnation by vote of the believers as a trivial thing,

24

the Lord has testified that this is nothing but the publication of his own sentence, and that what they have done on earth is ratified in heaven. For they have the Word of God to condemn the perverse; they have the Word of God to receive the penitent into grace.[41]

Church discipline is necessary[42]; it involves both private and public admonition,[43] sins that are both concealed and open,[44] and those that are relatively light and those that are extremely grave.[45] It has a threefold purpose: to exclude the infamous, to prevent the good people from being corrupted, and to produce repentance in those who are censured.[46]

In view of the grim reputation enjoyed by Calvin's Geneva, one of the surprising things about his treatment of church discipline in the *Institutes* is to discover how little he emphasized the *punitive* aspect, how strongly he emphasized that all discipline—even the solemn delivery to Satan—was essentially redemptive,[47] and his repeated warnings against too much rigor in the exercise of church censures.[48] Even the final act of excommunication was intended to be corrective rather than punitive:

> Accordingly, though ecclesiastical discipline does not permit us to live familiarly or have intimate contact with excommunicated persons, we ought nevertheless to strive by whatever means we can in order that they may turn to a more virtuous life and may return to the society and unity of the church. So the apostle also teaches: "Do not look upon them as enemies, but warn them as brothers" [II Thess. 3:15]. Unless this gentleness is maintained in both private and public censures, there is danger lest we soon slide down from discipline to butchery.[49]

This is the total of what is pertinent regarding Calvin's ecclesiology in the *Institutes,* and it reveals several basic principles regarding his view of the church, some of which are somewhat surprising.

1. Calvin had a strong view of the *jure divino* justification of the church itself, for the visible church was regarded as the mother of us all. But despite the consistorial form of organization in Geneva and the way in which later Reformed churches organized themselves and justified their polity, there is no attempt by Calvin to make a *jure divino* claim for any particular polity. He recommended the "assembly of Elders" *(Consensus seniorum)* as an ancient and useful form

of church order, but there is no hierarchy of church courts of the kind set up in Scotland or demanded by the Westminster Assembly as having clear scriptural authority.

2. He made a clear distinction between the features of the church that were instituted by Jesus and all other aspects of church life and worship that might be adopted by the church from time to time to minister to a particular age or nation. The former were to be regarded as permanent in the church, whereas the latter were regarded as variable.

3. At the center of the essential, dominical ordering of the church were the orders of the gospel ministry, the ministry of the Word. Indeed, when we study the way in which he suggests the church and its ministry must act in respect to church discipline, we can see that, to Calvin, the concept of ministry was central to the whole purpose and intention of church order.

4. For the rest, the basic principle was that anything that the church does and any forms that it adopts should be for the explicit purpose of edification and for good order. If it made for confusion rather than order, for show rather than edification, it was to be excluded. At this point, when Jesus had given us no explicit instructions, Calvin expected Christians to use their sanctified common sense.

At this point, for the sake of historical accuracy, we should note that the Ecclesiastical Ordinances of the city of Geneva, which were certainly inspired by Calvin's thought and issued with his authority, give evidence of a more presbyterial (collegial) form of church government.

In laying down the various orders of ministry in the Genevan church, the Ordinances speak of "the Third Order, Which is That of Elders, Who Are Called 'Commis,' of Those Delegated by the Seigneury to the Consistory."

Their office was "to watch over the life of each person, to admonish in a friendly manner those whom they see to be at fault and leading a disorderly life, and when necessary to report them to the Company [of pastors], who will be authorized to administer fraternal discipline and to do so in association with the elders."[50] Earlier in the Ordinances, however, the elders had been specifically recognized as "the Seigneury's delegates,"[51] as those designated as "commis" by the civil authority. This indicates the extent to which this particular order of government reflected the wishes of the Genevan civil government, and perhaps the extent to which the latter was determined to have some control over church affairs. Philip Hughes has pointed out that sometimes it was difficult to define the line of demarcation and authority between the civil and ecclesiastical authorities in the matter of excommunication.[52]

REFORMED CONFESSIONS

Much the same must be said for the Reformed confessions. Like the ancient creeds,[53] all the most important confessions that arose out of the Reformed churches state that the Holy Catholic Church is called into being by God, but they do not contain anything about its polity. Question 54 of the Heidelberg Catechism (1563) may be taken as typical. It occurs in the section on the Holy Spirit and, together with Question 55 on the Communion of Saints, is virtually all the Confession has to say on the church:

Q. 54: What do you believe concerning "the Holy Catholic Church"?

A: I believe that, from the beginning to the end of the world, and from among the whole human race, the Son of God, by his Spirit and his Word, gathers, protects, and preserves for himself, in the unity of the true faith, a congregation chosen for eternal life. Moreover, I believe that I am and forever will remain a living member of it.

Q. 55: What do you understand by "the communion of saints"?

A: First, that believers one and all, as partakers of the Lord Christ, and all his treasures and gifts, shall share in one fellowship. Second, that each one ought to know that he is obliged to use his gifts freely and with joy for the benefit and welfare of other members.[54]

Apart from the biblical references to support the answers, that is all. There is no suggestion that the church should be (or should not be) congregational, presbyterial, or even episcopal or papal, although because of the times in which they were written, there is a strong presumption in several of the confessions that the organization would not be papal.

This is true even of the *Scots Confession* of 1560. Chapter XVI on "The Kirk" has a strong emphasis on the unity and universality of the church, and if it has one distinctive feature, it is its emphasis on the church's purity as a communion of saints, pointing in the direction that was to be taken by the later Puritans.[55] Chapter XVIII deals with "The Notes by which the True Kirk Shall Be Determined From the False, and Who Shall Be Judge of Doctrine," in which the Confession could be expected to speak in somewhat extravagant terms of "the horrible harlot, the false Kirk," but it is here that, to the two marks of the church that had been specifically cited by Calvin—"the true preaching of the Word" and "the right administration of the sacraments"—the third mark, which was only implicit in the *Institutes,* was explicitly added—"ecclesiastical discipline uprightly administered."[56] For the rest, the confession claims that the individual parishes in Scotland were true churches in the sense of the true churches of the New Testament because they have the pure Word of God preached in them, and chapter XX on "General Councils" affirmed that, while councils were to be respected insofar as the doctrines they propounded could be substantiated by the Word of God, such councils could err and had erred. The only other passage dealing with the church is chapter XXV, which speaks of "The Gifts Freely Given to the Kirk" and stresses its eschatological character. But even in this most Scottish of all Confessions, *there is nothing about the Church's organization and polity.*[57]

The *Second Helvetic Confession* of 1566 is the longest of the early Reformed confessions, probably because it was consciously answering opponents on both the right and the left wings of the church, as Calvin had done. Furthermore, of all the confessions, it reveals most clearly the influence of Calvin's *Institutes.* Its statements on the church are to be found in chapter XVII, "Of the Catholic and Holy Church of God, and of the One Only Head of the Church,"[58] and chapter XVIII, "Of the Ministers of the Church, Their Institution and Duties."[59]

As in the other confessions, we find the same insistence on the oneness, catholicity, and unity of the church of Jesus Christ, and there is an important passage in which differences in the church were recognized, although its authors maintained that such differences did not destroy its essential unity.[60] In speaking of the signs and marks of the church, it stressed "the lawful and sincere preaching of the Word,"[61] and although outside the church there is no salvation, it declared that the church is not bound to its signs.

Nevertheless, by the signs [of the true church] mentioned above, we do not so narrowly restrict the Church as to teach that all those are outside the Church who either do not participate in the sacraments, at least not willingly and through contempt, but rather, being forced by necessity, unwillingly abstain from them or are deprived of them; or in whom faith sometimes fails, though it is not entirely extinguished and does not wholly cease; or in whom imperfections and errors due to weakness are found. For we know that God had some friends in the world outside the commonwealth of Israel.[62]

In the same way, the *Second Helvetic Confession* insisted that the Unity of the Church is not to be sought in external rites, but in its testimony to the historic faith.

We diligently teach that care is to be taken wherein the truth and unity of the Church chiefly lies, lest we rashly provoke and foster schisms in the Church. Unity consists not in outward rites and ceremonies, but rather in the truth and unity of the catholic faith. The catholic faith is not given to us by human laws, but by Holy Scriptures, of which the Apostles' Creed is a compendium.[63]

The importance of the Apostles' Creed here is that it shows that those who developed the Reformed Confessions had no intention of starting the church de novo. They wished to see the church reformed according to the truth of God's revelation in the scriptures, but falling in line with the apostolic tradition and within the historic faith.

But the most important section of this chapter on the church is its emphasis on the headship of Christ. The writers declared that the church cannot be governed by any other spirit than by the Spirit of Christ,[64] and although they may have forgotten it in later years, that remained at the heart of their ecclesiology: ecclesiology is also, in essence, pneumatology because it is the Spirit's primary function to point to Christ himself (John 16:13–16). If Christ is to be truly the Head of the church through his Spirit, then it should mean that we must never allow secondary forms of church government to prevent the Spirit from speaking his word to the church. The church can never become so incarcerated within its own *system* of government that it cannot be obedient and responsive.

Chapter XVIII of the *Confession* urged a proper respect for the church's ministry. It spoke of ministers as God's gift, of Christ as the great Teacher (and Pastor, cf. 5.131), of the various orders of ministry known to the New Testament, of the minister's calling and ordination, and of the nature of ministry within the New Testament church. It also spoke of the Priesthood of All Believers, of the powers of ministerial office, and of a minister's duties, especially in the exercise of church discipline. We should read this against the background of what Calvin had said about the pastoral intent of all church discipline.

However, there are a few sections in the chapter that have a more direct bearing on church polity.

The minister's call and election (5.150). In this section we see the shape of what could be a presbyterial order, or a form of church government by delegation, for in protesting against ill-equipped people usurping ministerial authority, it declared: "Let them [i.e., ministers] be carefully chosen by the Church or by those delegated from the Church for that purpose in a proper order without any uproar, dissension and rivalry."

The power in the minister's office (5.159). Looked at from the point of view of sixteenth-century prejudices about the prestige of clerical orders, or in terms of what ministers became in Protestantism, it is dangerous to speak of "power" in the minister's office. But the *Confession* is careful to distinguish this "power" from any thought of status. It declares:

And this is more like a service than a dominion. The Keys. For a lord gives up his power to the steward in his house, and for that cause gives him the keys, that he may admit into or exclude from the house those whom his lord will have admitted or excluded. In virtue of this power the minister, because of his office, does that which the Lord has commanded him to do; and the Lord confirms what he does, and wills that what his servant has done will be so regarded and acknowledged, as if he himself had done it.

The essential equality of ministers (5.160). There is no need to comment much on this. The *Confession* urges that "the one and an equal function is given to all ministers in the Church," and the gospel principle that the leader among Christ's people ought to "become as one who serves [Luke 22:26]" had obvious implications for the church's polity.

The necessity for preserving order in the church (5.161). We have already seen that concern for due order in church worship and government was a primary emphasis in Calvin's view of the church; but it was clearly incorporated into Reformed churchmanship not because it was one of Calvin's ideas, but because it was an important principle in the apostolic church.

Synods (5.167). Perhaps the section most directly related to what was later recognized as presbyterian polity is the section on synods; but when we read that section carefully, it appears that synods were to be regarded not so much as part of a hierarchy of church courts, but as a means whereby ministers might mutually hold one another under the church's discipline.

> Nevertheless, there ought to be proper discipline among ministers. In synods the doctrine and life of ministers is to be carefully examined. Offenders who can be cured are to be rebuked by the elders and restored to the right way, and if they are incurable, they are to be deposed, and like wolves driven away from the flock of the Lord by the true shepherds. For, if they be false teachers, they are not to be tolerated at all. Neither do we disapprove of ecumenical councils, if they are convened according to the example of the apostles, for the welfare of the church and not for its destruction.

All these passages had implications for the Reformed understanding of the church and its polity, and it is clear that adherents of both the polities that emerged later out of Calvinism could have fully endorsed them. Despite its length and thoroughness in the treatment of the church, the *Second Helvetic Confession said nothing explicitly about polity,* and if presbyterian polity became virtually the accepted form of government in a majority of the Reformed churches, its actual roots may have to be sought more in its social and political connections at that time, and in the principle of "good order," than in any claim to *jus divinum.*

A note about the *Westminster Confession*[65] should be inserted here because, although it was not properly a confession that arose out of the European Reformed churches that immediately contribute to our tradition, it was regarded as one of the best of those confessions in its time and was accepted by the New England Congregationalists.[66] Indeed it is worth noting that the Congregationalists in the assembly, while remaining "Dissenting Brethren" with regard to the polity enjoined by Westminster, participated fully in producing the confession itself and the rest of the Westminister Standards.

In view of the importance of the ecclesiological issue in the debates of the assembly—it had, after all, been the explicit reason for the assembly's call in 1642—we might, at first sight, be somewhat surprised to find relatively little about the church and its polity in the *Westminster Confession.* This is because the assembly's work on church government had already been issued in a separate document, *The Form of Government;* and if the statements on that subject in the *Confession* (chapters XXV, "Of the Church"; XXVI, "Of the Communion of Saints"; XXX, "Of Church Censures"; and XXXI, "Of Synods and Councils")[67] stop short of the rigid presbyterianism argued in the assembly, it is probably because it was intended to be a document to which all members of the assembly could subscribe, and there had been some hope that the majority would be able to persuade the Dissenters to accept the form of government they had presented. As it is, there is nothing in those chapters on the church, censures, synods, and councils that most of the leaders in New England could not wholeheartedly endorse and in fact they did endorse the doctrinal parts.[68]

The records also show that, perhaps unlike most of their European counterparts, the Scots Commissioners at Westminster firmly believed that the presbyterian order of church government was *jure divino* and actively worked to get that theological position accepted by the assembly. Moreover, one of them, Robert Baillie, was continually involved in getting continental theologians to write in favor of the Scottish position as a counterbalance to any appeal the Congregationalists might make to the practice of New England; this politicking may be one reason why *jure divino* presbyterianism began to appear on the continent of Europe at this time.

In the event, the Scots were successful in getting all four parts of their projected uniformity in religion through the assembly and the English Parliament—the form of church government, directory of worship, catechism, and confession of faith—and it was so much in agreement with Scottish presbyterian practice that the decisions of the English Westminster Assembly were accepted almost without alteration by the Scottish General Assembly and Parliament. Indeed, the ecclesiological and theological work of the assembly had only temporary effect in England, whereas it had an ongoing effect in Scotland. At only one point did the Scots fail to get their way—the English Parliament was willing to establish the presbyterian system in the Church of England, but only on its own authority: it was unwilling to grant that the system of church government was so clearly to be found in scripture that it and it alone could claim divine right. Yet the Scots did manage to persuade a good number of the English divines, and in 1646 the ministers of London published the book that set out to prove that position, *Jus Divinum Regiminis Ecclesiastici, or the Divine Right of Church-Government, asserted and evidenced by the Holy Scriptures.* It seems clear that before this date, *jure divino* presbyterianism had first appeared among the Scots and was advanced in the writings of men like George Gillespie, Robert Baillie, and Samuel Rutherford (all of whom were Commissioners to Westminster) and in the writings of those Reformed divines on the Continent whom the Scots had been able to persuade to endorse their cause.[69]

CONGREGATIONAL ECCLESIOLOGY

Although all the views on ecclesiology that go into our church tradition are essentially biblical, Puritan Congregationalism appears to have been the only one that has centered in polity and that claimed, from the first, to be *jure divino.* Perhaps this is why one has the impression that congregationalists of all sorts tend to remain fundamentalist in matters of polity long after they have ceased to be fundamentalist in anything else.

If we are to do justice to the tradition, however, we have to see it as a reaction to the ecclesiastical and political context out of which it arose. By enforcing the *legal* requirement of their subjects obeying the ecclesiastical laws of the crown, the Tudors and Stuarts in England practically forced Separatists and Puritans to regard the Bible as a book of law that had precedence over the law of the land and that, in turn, caused the Bible to be treated more and more literally: legalism produced literalism in reaction.[70] In respect to the doctrine of the Church, Perry Miller's words about the Separatists were equally true of the non-separating Puritans, "since those [biblical] rules were held to be explicit and all-sufficient, and were to be administered only by God's chosen people, there would be complete unanimity."[71]

Robert Baillie was perfectly justified in pointing to the similarities between the ecclesiology of the Congregationalists in the assembly (or Independents, as he preferred to call them) and that of the earlier Separatists.[72] The "Independents" *did* allow a stronger persuasive authority to synods and church councils, and they *did* maintain their essential relationship to the national church, but in the first case the authority was still *persuasive,* and in the second case the relationship to the Church of England became academic when their churches were removed the breadth of the Atlantic from the bishops. We must recognize that there has been a "congregational" form of church-manship that has persistently arisen in the church history among those who go to the Bible in a simple literal way. Congregational restorationism has been a characteristic not only of Separatists and Puritans, but also in later history, where one finds it recurring in the restorationist movements of the American frontier and in such sects as the Plymouth Brethren in England.

Not that the Congregational Puritans had any intention of being sectarian in their churchmanship. In *An Apologeticall Narration* (1643–44) they set down the method they had followed and the principles they had adopted in arriving at their ecclesiology. The Apologists said that at first they were concerned only with the negative aspects of churchmanship, the ways in which they believed that the form and worship of the Church of England were not true to the biblical pattern, but they then recognized their need to find out what ought to be the true form of the church:

> We were cast upon a farther necessity of enquiring into and view-ing the *light part,* the positive part of *Church-worship* and Govern-ment; and to that end to search out what were the first Apostoli-que directions, pattern and examples of those Primitive Churches recorded in the New Testament, as that sacred pillar of fire to guide us. And in this enquirie, we lookt upon the word of Christ as impartially, and unprejudicedly, as men of flesh and blood are like to doe in any juncture of time that may fall out.[73]

They declared that their primary authority outside themselves "was the Primitive patterns and example of the churches erected by the Apostles. Our consciences were possessed with that reverence and adoration of the fulness of the Scriptures, as to make *man of God perfect,* so also to make the Churches of God perfect, . . . if the directions and examples therein were fully known and followed." They admitted that they might not have had a perfect answer to all the problems of church organization and worship, but they claimed that they had had enough to go on, "and the observation of so many particulars to be laid forth in the Word, became to us a more certaine evidence and cleare confirmation that there were the like rules and ruled cases for all occasions whatsoever, if we were able to discerne them."[74]

In that sense they were clearly restorationists. But they main-tained that there was one principle that prevented this Restora-tionism from becoming static and unchangeable. They said that where they found no clear scriptural evidence, they suspended final judgment "untill God should give us further light."[75] They said that they had had too much evidence of their own earlier error in regard to their conformity with the established church to regard their present findings as absolute; and therefore they had reserved to themselves the right of changing their opinion, "though not lightly," whenever it could be shown that they had adopted any practice through a misunderstanding of the scriptural rule.[76] In that way we may say that they understood the ongoing guidance of the Holy Spirit in their approach to scripture, which prevented them casting their present interpretation of the scriptural pattern into a permanent and unalterable ecclesiology.

The same general purpose, to restore as much of the New Testament pattern of the church as possible, was the intention of the Puritans in New England, and the books of John Cotton show that the New Englanders shared almost unanimous agreement with their friends in the Westminster Assembly. At only one point was there any material difference—the attitude to religious toleration—and as Perry Miller has shown, on this matter the New Englanders suffered from having carried with them the prejudices current in England during the 1630s when they emigrated. Had they experienced the problems of the English civil war, they might have come to a radically different view, as the Dissenting Brethren had done.

What, then, are we to learn and take from this Congregational tradition, which, within the American context, is perhaps the most venerable aspect of Protestant ecclesiastical history within this nation?

1. First, let us admit that we are far less convinced than the Puritans or their opponents that there is but one form of the church presented to us in the New Testament, or that a careful study of the scriptures will reveal a single authoritative pattern of church government and worship. Regarding the various polities, B.H. Streeter once observed that it reminded him of the remark of the queen in one of Lewis Carroll's books: "They have all won and they shall all have prizes."[77]

We agree that the Holy Catholic Church itself is *jure divino* and that it exists by divine institution, but in the area of government it appears from the New Testament evidence that the Holy Spirit may organize the church differently in order to be a faithful witness to the gospel in the time and place where it has to make its testimony. Negatively we have to say that the attempt to restore the New

Testament pattern of the church absolutely and in detail can result in a static form of the church that refuses to adapt itself according to the changing needs of the gospel.

2. Second, although the Puritan forebears of New England may sometimes have been guilty of that, they did own a dynamic principle that pointed in a different direction. John Robinson, the pastor of the Pilgrim church before it left Leyden, had laid down this principle in a sermon preached to the Pilgrims at the time of their emigration. Edward Winslowe said that Robinson used these words, or "to the same purpose":

> We are now ere long to part asunder, and the Lord knoweth whether ever he should live to see our faces again: but whether the Lord had appointed it or not, he charged us before God and his blessed Angels, to follow him no further than he followed Christ. And if God should reveal any thing to us by any other instrument of his, to be as ready to receive it, as ever we were to receive any truth by his Ministery: For he was very confident the Lord had more truth and light yet to breake forth out of his holy Word. He took occasion also miserably to bewaile the state and condition of the Reformed Churches, who were come to a period in Religion, and would goe no further than the instruments of their Reformation: As for example, the *Lutherans* they could not be drawne to goe beyond what *Luther* saw, for whatever part of God's will he had further imparted and revealed to *Calvin*, they will rather die than embrace it. And so also, saith he, you see the *Calvinists*, they stick where he left them: A misery much to bee lamented; For though they were precious shining lights in their times, yet God had not revealed his whole will to them: And were they now living, saith hee, they would bee as ready and willing to embrace further light, as that they had received. Here also he put us in mind of our Church-Covenant (at least that part of it) whereby wee promise and covenant with God and one with another, to receive whatsoever light or truth shall be made known to us from his written Word: but withall exhorted us to take heed what we received for truth, and well to examine and compare, and weigh it with other Scriptures of truth, before we received it; For, saith he, *It is not possible the Christian world should come so lately out of such thick Antichristian darknesse, and that full perfection of knowledge should breake forth at once.*[78]

This is the principle of *semper reformanda,* which is fundamentally theological: it is a threat only to those who would prefer that Pentecost had never happened and who think of God as essentially

36

static. Whatever the changelessness of God may mean, it can never mean that. John Robinson pointed to the followers of the Reformers who were unwilling to go any further than they had gone, which was, in his view, something to be deplored. But he had asserted that there was "more light and truth yet to breake forth out of [God's] holy Word," and he asked his followers to follow his own instructions no more than they saw that he had followed Christ's.

This principle recognizes that at the heart of New Testament church practice there is the dynamic leading of the Holy Spirit. Pentecost is at the center of the New Testament, and although the Spirit does not lead the church in such a way as would contradict the revelation of scripture, it can and does reveal new insights as to how the mind of Christ is to be discovered and obeyed in our own time.

3. The centrality of the doctrine of the Holy Spirit in relationship to what the New Testament had to say about Jesus Christ could radically modify the literalism of restorationist ecclesiology. It is seen in the Puritans' distinction between magisterial power (appropriate to the state) and ministerial authority (which alone is appropriate in the church). Their insistence that authority in the church is purely spiritual, and therefore noncoercive, is grounded in this New Testament insight. To put the principle into modern terms, the only authority appropriate to the church of Jesus Christ is government that manifests the Spirit of Christ. This is a fundamental insight on which we would have to insist in any ecumenical expression of unity, for it is not sufficient that the church be shown to be visibly united, but it must also be clear that it is united in the Spirit of love that was in our Lord.

4. Finally, is there anything to be learned from restorationism itself—from the attempt to restore the New Testament pattern of the church?

There is the obvious negative lesson of the exclusivism and danger of absolutizing one particular form and polity, but there is a positive lesson that the recurring theme of restorationism in church history teaches us. Every restorationist movement has arisen in protest against churches that have become infiltrated by the culture, and that have allowed the forms of the dominant society to dictate their own forms of practice and government. The New Testament church did not, but its ways of worship and government were taken from our Lord himself and from his living Spirit at the heart of its gospel and mission.

Restorationism, and not least the kind of restorationism of our own Puritan heritage, reminds us that the form of the church *matters,* that the way in which the church is organized, the spirit of its worship, and the instrumentalities of its life and government *are a visible testimony to the seriousness with which the church treats its own gospel.* Church government is either an indispensable testimony to the way the gospel is to be lived in community, and to the priorities of the gospel, or it becomes a visible denial of the very gospel we profess. This is a fundamental insight toward which, in a limited and imperfect way, the Puritans were pointing us.

New England ecclesiology has a particular significance when we see it in terms of Ernst Troeltsch's typology. Troeltsch undoubtedly set out to develop a sociology of religion, and although his book hardly achieved that, he did manage to produce a significant typology of Christian churchmanship.[79] Looking at the whole sweep of Christian history, Troeltsch discerned three distinctive types of churchmanship that have developed at different times and in response to different circumstances; the church type, the sect type, and what, for want of a better name, he called the "third" type. As I have pointed out elsewhere, there seems to be a distinct correlation between Troeltsch's three types and the three fundamental channels of authority that the churches have recognized throughout their history.[80] It is the first two of these, however, that are particularly significant in New England ecclesiology.

The church type has developed whenever there is a close association between an established church and a particular state. It was to be seen as a result of the Constantinian Settlement of religion, and it was also in evidence in the ecclesiastical settlements of the Reformation. The church type affirms the society in which it is set and assumes pastoral responsibility for the whole of it. It is therefore organized geographically (dioceses or synods and parishes). It receives the individual member as an infant in baptism and nurtures that individual through its sacraments until the Christian offices associated with death. Such a view of the church works for the achievement of the kingdom of God in history, and the nurturing may be achieved mainly by its education. The government of such a church is inevitably clerical and professional.

The sect type is very much a reaction to this kind of churchmanship, since it is clear that the clerical leaders of church-type churches often become too identified with the society in which they serve, and too ready to maintain the status quo at all costs. The sect type tends to withdraw from this world, to emphasize a salvation and a kingdom that is eschatological, and is concerned by its proclamation of the gospel to reclaim as many as possible out of this world into the church. It emphasizes the Bible and tries to restore the purity that was in the church of the New Testament. It is "prophetic" in its ministry. As Troeltsch himself said:

> Whereas the Church assumes the objective concrete holiness of the sacerdotal office, of Apostolic Succession, of the *Depositum fidei* and of the sacraments, and appeals to the extension of the Incarnation which takes place permanently through the priesthood, the sect, on the other hand, appeals to the ever new common performance of the moral demands, which, at bottom, are founded only upon the Law and the Example of Christ. In this, it must be admitted that they are in direct contact with the Teaching of Jesus. . . . Scripture history and the history of the Primitive Church are permanent ideals, to be accepted in their literal sense, not the starting-point, historically limited and defined, for the development of the church.[81]

The significance of this for the ecclesiology of the UCC is that the positive aspects of both the church type and the sect type may be claimed as part of our oldest heritage. Thus our churches have been world-affirming in the sense that they have wished to take responsibility for all people in the society where they are set, and offer pastoral help wherever it is needed. At the same time we would not wish to deny the gathered church's emphasis on the New Testament as providing the ethical norm for Christian behavior in church and society. I suggest that the very ambivalence of New England Congregationalism in this respect may be an asset rather than a liability.

Chapter 4
Assessment of Traditional Ecclesiologies

In this chapter I attempt to pull together the results of the discussion of the traditional ecclesiologies that have gone into the common tradition of the United Church of Christ, for it is clear that some things should be learned from the study of how our forebears[1] thought of the church.

Walter Marshall Horton made a statement that became a truism for the ecumenical movement. He told me that the primary effect of joining the ecumenical movement is to make everyone *more,* not less, conscious of one's own special loyalties and traditions.[2] The same thing should have been true for churches that try to express the ecumenical idea, such as the UCC, and I fear that one of the reasons we have failed to make the kind of ecumenical impact that we should have made has been our failure to take our traditions with due seriousness. As a result our "ecumenism" has seemed to be simply a matter of practical expediency or union for the sake of being bigger, whereas originally it arose out of our essential theology: that is, it arose originally out of our fundamental beliefs about God, about God's good news in Jesus Christ, and about the church's mission. We shall continue to be frustrated from making the kind of contribution we could make to the ecumenical understanding of the church until we are prepared to give as much serious study to our constituent ecclesiologies as Roman Catholics, Anglo-Catholics, Lutherans, or Baptists are prepared to give to their own.

HOW FAR ARE OUR TRADITIONAL ECCLESIOLOGIES STILL VALID?

When we ask ourselves how far our traditional ecclesiologies are still valid, it is clear that few ministers and still fewer church members regard them as valid at all. Most church members have not been instructed about the form of the church, or even in why we believe our ecumenical form is important. Perhaps the first thing we have to learn from our forebears, in this respect, is that the church *matters,* that it is not simply a voluntary society like a service club or a social club for wine and cheese parties, but that it is the community of those who have been called *out* of the world by God to be God's community *in* the world.

I suspect that for the majority of our adherents the traditional doctrines of the church are not in the slightest bit valid. But if this is true, it should be for the right and not the wrong reasons. We may properly question the older views about the church because they no longer enable us to proclaim the gospel in our day as they assisted our ancestors to proclaim it in theirs; or because the gospel we proclaim is broader than the exclusivism that regarded itself as utterly right and damned everyone else; or because we have reached insights into biblical faith that demand something different. We may *not* properly question the older views because we prefer something more like a country club, or more like a political party, or more like a society for studying anything but the Bible. This does not mean that I am against friendliness, or against proper social action, or against studying anything *but* the Bible, but we do have to get our priorities straight.

One of the reasons we cannot simply appropriate our older ecclesiologies for use today is because they arose out of social contexts that were very different from our own, and therefore spoke to societies very different from the one in which we are called to bear witness. It is not that our gospel has changed, but that it demands radically different forms in which to challenge the people of this century and this culture. And if the *shape* of the church matters, if, as I have suggested, the way in which it organizes and governs itself is an integral part of the gospel and a visible example of Christian community, then the forms and instrumentalities adopted in the sixteenth and seventeenth centuries need some revision.

For example, how many of us have reflected that until the end of the last century, most people lived in relatively rural areas? Until the development of the railroad and modern communications, most people remained relatively static throughout their lives, and probably a majority would never travel more than thirty miles away from home—the distance to the nearest market town. These are generalizations, but they nevertheless remain generally true. Now compare the kind of church that would be appropriate to a rural, close-knit community, in which everyone had known everyone else for as long as they could remember, with the kind of church that is needed in a large urban area, where the congregation is constantly shifting and where one has to make friends quickly before departing to mount the next rung up the corporate ladder. Or compare the kind of church life that was possible when everyone felt safe to go to church any evening with the church that has to minister in areas where the population locks itself into little private castles each night for fear of being mugged. How does our ecclesiology meet our new urban setting, with its anonymity, speed of movement, and shifting membership? How do its forms and ways of organizing itself testify to the gospel that we have to proclaim to such a society?

We might make a similar point with regard to the world outreach of the church. Our forebears in the faith were probably much more conscious of the rest of the world than we are in some ways because, at least in the nineteenth century, the churches throughout the Anglo-Saxon world became wholeheartedly involved in missionary work. But it was a patronizing and imperial kind of involvement, and today we would not make that mistake. That is, we would not make it *if* we were to get involved on a global scale; but I suspect that our churches are today much more concerned with the church in the USA than they are with maintaining a Christian witness in other countries. Yet every newscast shows us that we belong to an ever-shrinking world and that we cannot exclude success or failure elsewhere from affecting ourselves. Our present ecclesiology, even our ecumenical ecclesiology (COCU), virtually stops at the Atlantic and Pacific seaboards. Yet everything else we see and read should be telling us that national churches, like national states, can no longer afford to act unilaterally, or as if they were self-contained.

But when we have made due allowance for the ways in which our older ecclesiologies cannot simply be taken over in the form they assumed in earlier centuries, what are the positive insights that still retain validity for us?

1. From the Reformation of Luther—the *Evangelische* tradition—

there is the insight, which must surely be central to any concept of the church, that God's grace is central and that we are justified by faith. There is also the emphasis on the authority of the Bible, not indeed in any slavish or literalistic way, but because this is the record of the way God has dealt with us in Jesus Christ. We have faith in *this* God who revealed the divine nature in this way and whose actions have been set down by these people in the Bible. So, too, our churchmanship will have to acknowledge the priesthood of all believers, not because it happens to catch the fancy of a democratically ordered society, but because it reflects the fundamental insight of the church described in the New Testament.

2. From the "Christian" tradition we see the importance of holding loose to our previous preconceptions and prejudices as we address ourselves to the task of evangelizing our society. This was the characteristic of religion on the American frontier, and we have to recognize that, despite all its shortcomings and even crudities, it was this same kind of frontier religion that most civilized America and enabled it to enter so soon upon its international role. This tradition also suggests that evangelism is not a matter to be left to professionals, but is a call to every member and each Christian community. We also have to learn from these frontier "Christians" that the goal of the church is ecumenical; our aim is not to be distinctive as a particular denomination, with identifiable characteristics and beliefs, but to be "Christian." Granted it may be impossible—and even undesirable—to lose a denominational character in the present state of American pluralism, the ultimate goal is simply to acknowledge our membership in the church of Jesus Christ, to be Christian.

3. The classic Reformed tradition stands at the heart of our history and our theological heritage, and it reinforces many of the aspects of churchmanship that were to be found in Luther; the Centrality of Grace, Justification by Faith, *sola scriptura,* and the Priesthood of All Believers are all Protestant insights that Reformed people have cherished.

But to them we must add, first, an integrated theology. What we say about the church is not added to what we say about the rest of Christian doctrine, but is an extension of it. This surely was the great contribution that came from Calvin and that was expressed in the Reformed Confessions. Here we see an ecclesiology being developed that was consistent with what was being said about Jesus Christ, the Trinity, the Holy Spirit, etc., and although the system of government may have reflected, to some extent, the social prejudices of that time—the "aristocratic" or oligarchic principle preferred in Switzerland, Holland, Scotland, and parts of Germany—there can be little doubt that it represented an integral and integrated part of Reformed doctrine.

But unlike the Scottish Presbyterianism of the Westminster Assembly, Calvin and the Confessions did not represent the presbyterian system as *jure divino*. Indeed, Calvin was careful in the *Institutes* to distinguish what he believed to be of divine institution and what he regarded as matters of practical expediency for the good order of the church. It should be noted that both he and the Confessions stop far short of claiming the whole presbyterian system, the *hierarchy* of church courts, as of divine institution.

We should see from this that *practicality* had a place in the Reformed system of churchmanship. Whatever helped the church to be organized in a way that made for decency and good order was regarded by Calvin with approval. But the practical goals of the church were not to be pursued for their own sake, but because they were vitally important to the church's ministry and mission. This was the real goal of any practical measures taken for the church.

This should cause us to focus on a basic insight of Reformed churchmanship—the church is *semper reformanda,* always being reformed: there is within this the conviction and, we would hope, the readiness to accept the Holy Spirit's leading into new truth as it is revealed to the church in God's Word.

4. The Congregationalists were the only group within the Reformed family that may be said to have had their raison d'être in their polity, but here again we must be careful how we interpret this. The crucial step that was taken was that of trying to restore the apostolic church of the New Testament *in detail* and to reestablish that system of order and government in the seventeenth century, but they recognized that the Bible did not always provide them with detailed answers to all their problems.

The interesting reason they stopped short of Presbyterianism and ended by stressing the autonomy of the local congregation was because, although they could prove the existence of local congregations in the New Testament and that those congregations had the power of disciplining recalcitrant members, they could not prove those powers for a church council or synod: in the New Testament such "councils" were not engaged in anything but doctrinal matters (cf. Acts 15) and did not carry more than advisory, spiritual authority. So the same concern that prevented Calvin and the writers of the

Confessions from claiming a *jure divino* basis for their consistorial order and caused them to insist that some aspects of church order were simply practical for preventing scandal and for better administration, caused the Congregational Puritans to reject *jure divino* Presbyterianism. If we recognize that there was a similar concern, even though it caused two groups within the Reformed family to turn in different directions, it could be a way through the impasse of owning both polities in our history.

Congregationalists also carried the doctrine of the Priesthood of All Believers to the point where every member of the church was brought into serious pastoral relationship with every other member. It was a form of church government in which (although for nurture and edification the distinction between a minister and the people was still maintained) a concept of *mutual ministry* was made real.

The strong emphasis on claiming *jus divinum* in the church only for those aspects of church government that could be directly proved from the New Testament prevented them (at least in England) from claiming the coercive power of the state, or assuming a coercive power in the church, even on the grounds of practicality and good order. Unfortunately this was not always true in the churches of New England, as the stories of Anne Hutchinson, Roger Williams, the Quakers, and the Baptists make clear. In England the pressures of the civil war made a different story, and I would maintain that that story was closer to their essential theological principles.

Closely allied to this latter point was the recognition of the Pentecost center to the New Testament. They, too, believed in *ecclesia semper reformanda*.

Moreover, ecclesiastical government was to be "according to the mind of Christ," which was revealed by the Holy Spirit, and the Holy Spirit was manifested predominantly in the gift of love. Once this is recognized as the central principle of church government, the church must be governed basically by the spirit of Christian persuasion and cannot allow the intrusion of secular coercion.

Although restorationism itself demands separate treatment, we must note that *any* attempt to restore the apostolic pattern of churchmanship is a practical confession that *the form of the church matters:* it is an acknowledgment that the way in which the church is governed is an integral testimony to what it proclaims and to the truth or falsehood of its claims.

THE LESSONS OF NEW TESTAMENT RESTORATIONISM

An essential truth is to be learned from all forms of New Testament restorationism: that just as the way in which the church operated and was governed in apostolic times became an essential testimony to the Spirit that controlled it and to the living Christ it proclaimed, so restorationism reminds us that we cannot ignore the form the church takes in our own day or the way it operates in society. All over the world, and particularly in the Third World, the cry has gone up that the actions of the Christian church must match its proclamation of Christ if it is to have any hope of being heard.

The church must learn from its own history, and one of the most obvious lessons from that history during the past 500 years arises from the recurring attempts to restore the church in its pristine New Testament pattern. This seems to occur whenever the contemporary church has strayed so far from the apostolic pattern that it has become a virtual denial of the gospel it is entrusted to proclaim. There should be a proper place for church tradition and a proper respect due to the church's leaders, but when these are accented to the point of causing the church's apostolic simplicity to be hidden, there is need for change. And where else are simple believers to find an authentic and authoritative form of the church to follow than in the church of the New Testament?

It is particularly important that this lesson should be taken to heart by those individuals or churches that actively seek the unity of the church to be expressed in a visible form. A form of visible unity established for its own sake, or one that prevents the church of the future from being obedient to the demands of the gospel, will almost inevitably engender a new Restorationist Reformation. We have to be extremely careful in church union negotiations not to make unity the goal, but to insist that unity is only the means whereby the church may be more *obedient*. And we have also to insist that not the slightest excuse or opportunity remains in the united church for the clerical arrogance or ecclesiastical triumphalism that makes radical reform a necessity for the church. Somehow the essential flexibility of church order that enables the church in later ages to adapt itself in faithfulness to the gospel's demands has to be guaranteed. Otherwise, there are bound to be further attempts from within the community of faith to restore the church's New Testament purity.

However, any attempt to restore the New Testament pattern of the church inevitably produces its own problems. The Bible is now available to all people—the simplest as well as the wisest. There is an inevitable tendency for simple but sincere people to interpret its words and forms without reference to their context and in the most literal way[3]; when this kind of simplistic interpretation gains sufficient following, the result is often a new sect that discards the larger part of Christian history and tries to establish the church de novo. Instead of reforming the church, it tries to re-form it. It is impossible to do that without discarding a great deal of the Holy Spirit's work in history, and therefore a great deal of invaluable Christian testimony. Even in times of greatest darkness and oppression we recognize the testimony of saints and martyrs, and there has been the faithful transmission of the gospel in unexpected places. One cannot deny the history of that witness without denying something that is part of the gospel itself.

There is also the tendency among all restorationists to regard their own interpretation of the New Testament evidence as absolute and divinely instituted. And that, too, is dangerous. It is true that those churches that have taken their stand basically on the New Testament pattern have generally agreed about the shape of the church and the pattern of its ministry; but there have also been significant differences or there would have been no distinctive denominations like Baptists, Disciples, Churches of Christ, Plymouth Brethren, Assemblies of God, Presbyterians, or Congregationalists. The existence of denominations that take their stand on biblical restorationism and yet differ among themselves clearly indicates that to follow the literal scriptures alone does not guarantee unity: some further canons of interpretation are needed. Otherwise, the church that results is likely to be the most exclusive and unecumenical church because its standards will not allow any modification.

Within the traditions that have made up the UCC there have fortunately been other principles that kept the churches from falling into the error of absolutizing their restorationist tendencies; otherwise, the UCC could not have happened. (Of course, there is another way of interpreting our history; there *are* those who think that it happened because the churches that constitute the UCC no longer cared sufficiently for their own traditions. But such people face the dilemma of owning an ecclesiology that condemns them virtually to permanent sectarianism.) Some examples of the modifying factors will be sufficient; the evangelical experience of frontier religion practically forced those who shared it to recognize conversion experience in others, even when those others belonged to different denominations. The ecumenical movement as we know it was born out of that Pietist breakthrough. In the classic Reformed tradition there was the reserve that we find in Calvin as to what could actually be regarded as of divine institution regarding the government of the church, and his consequent emphasis on practical good sense in the name of good order. In the Congregational tradition, in which the restorationist element was perhaps originally most pronounced, there was still a reluctance to make their immediate understanding of the scriptural evidence a binding rule for the future, and their insistence that the apostolic church must be governed by the apostolic spirit.

The Congregational experience offers a distinct ray of ecumenical hope. It underlines a curious feature of sincere restorationism that has not been given the attention it deserves. The more seriously biblical literalism is taken by its exponents, the more those who follow that course are undermining the very process in which they are engaged; for sooner or later any serious student of the New Testament is bound to come up against the dynamic fact of Pentecost and the centrality of the principle that the church has inherited an ongoing, controlling Spirit, whose primary gift is to interpret and reinterpret the scriptural record in a way that reveals Jesus Christ, and according to Christ's spirit of love and compassion. Literalism cannot finally stand against that discovery.

It is true that the Holy Spirit does not contradict the Word in scripture, that it points to the same Christ who is recorded in scripture, and that in this sense we can continue to speak of "Jesus Christ, the same yesterday, today and for ever." But it is the very *permanence* of that eternal Word of God in Christ that demands constant reinterpretation when the gospel is being presented to the successive ages of history and the ever-changing features of society. The same is true when the meaning of that eternal gospel is related to the institutional forms of church order and organization. It seems that there must have been a special Providence that permitted the ancient creeds, and many of the later confessions, to assert the divine institution of the church itself *without* tying the gospel to a particular form of government or polity. This does not mean that ecclesiastical polity is irrelevant, but that it must be continually open and subject to the guidance of the Holy Spirit.

ECCLESIOLOGY AND THE NEED FOR BASIC AUTHORITY

All this suggests that before we can deal properly with the shape of the church for our own time, we have to deal honestly with the need to define the basic authority (or authorities) on which it is based.

Peter Taylor Forsyth saw the need in 1905, when he said that there was "no question so deep and urgent at this moment as that regarding the seat of authority and its nature,"[4] and two years later, in addressing the divinity students at Yale in his Lyman Beecher Lectures, he declared:

> The question of ultimate authority for mankind is the greatest of all questions to meet the west, since the Catholic Church lost its place in the sixteenth century, and since criticism no longer allows the Bible to occupy that place. Yet the gospel of the future must come with the note of authority. Every challenge of authority but develops the need of it.[5]

Forsyth saw the issue in far broader dimensions than those of the church itself: it was for him the root problem of Western civilization. The events of our own century indicate that he may have been a prophet in that, for it is clear that there is no universally accepted system of ethics to which the armed might of communism, fascism, and secularized West, militant Israel, and militant Islam will all give allegiance. Moreover, it is clear that within the de-Christianization of our own Western societies, there is little that restrains the descent into terrorism and anarchy when the self-interest of particular groups is not held in check.

But although Forsyth correctly saw the issue in wider terms than the church, the lack of a clearly understood spiritual authority on which to base our ecclesiology is obviously a concern in defining our personal relationship to the church. We cannot any longer appeal in the absolute way we did to the authority of the church and its hierarchy, or the literal provisions of the scriptures, and in the light of modern psychology, we cannot place too much weight on our own religious experience. In any case, that would not convince anyone else. Nor will pure rationalism serve because if the church points to the eternal gospel of Jesus Christ, the authority on which it takes its form must find its basis in authority that is recognizably "Christian."

49

Indeed, the basic problem of our ecclesiology points to the problem at the heart of the faith crisis. Because we can no longer refer to the church's hierarchy, or to the Bible, or to the evangelical experience, or to our reason in the absolute ways we did in the past, we are left with a number of confluent testimonies. We are called to recognize that these point to the same truth, but we are called to walk toward that horizon in faith. And that was a basic insight to be learned from the Reformers.

Chapter 5
The Old and the New

When the UCC came into existence in 1957, it did so without any detailed doctrine of the church or commitment to any particular polity. At the time this was variously regarded as a supreme example of courageous ecumenism or a prize example of consummate folly and theological laxity. In the event, I believe that it was all these things.

It was an action of courageous ecumenism by two denominations in declaring that the principle of unity in the church of Jesus Christ was a priority that would not allow the acrimonies of theological debate to destroy or even hinder it. It is fairly stated in #1 of the Preamble to the *Constitution and Bylaws:*[1]

> The United Church of Christ, formed June 25th, 1957, by the union of the Evangelical and Reformed Church and The General Council of the Congregational Christian Churches of the United States in order to express more fully the oneness in Christ of the churches composing it, to make more effective their common witness in Him, and to serve His kingdom in the world, hereby adopts this constitution.

This was certainly an act of faith and courage, and in those days of "biblical theology" few persons doubted that the UCC either could or would then address itself to working out the theological basis on which this new and exciting expression of Christian unity had been established. There was, after all, essential agreement in all matters of theology between such people as the Niebuhrs and Elmer Arndt on the one hand and Douglas Horton, Gerald Cragg, and John Bennett on the other. It was the period when there was a real ecumenical consensus in theology based on a new discovery of the Bible, and the thrust of that biblical faith was beautifully expressed in what is still the best and briefest of all twentieth-century creedal statements, our own Statement of Faith. Give us a little time, it was assumed, and we shall soon produce an ecclesiology to match our ecumenical conviction about the nature of the church.

But this theological undergirding never took place. A note of personal reminiscence must be inserted here. At the first meeting of the Theological Commission, the chairman, Douglas Horton, went round the table and asked the members what they thought should be the immediate task of that commission. I (greatly daring, as only a recently arrived member of the UCC) ventured to suggest that we should address ourselves to the nature of the church and its ministry. The suggestion was received with considerable support by the members of that commission, but before we could begin any serious work on it, we were flooded with a series of comparatively trivial issues that, we were assured, needed our immediate attention. The longer this continued, the less likely we were to deal with that basic theological issue, for as we progressed into the 1960s, the whole climate within our denomination shifted from concern about the church to concern with the world.

Much of that concern with the issues of society was certainly needed, and yet . . . what *was* the United Church of Christ? *Why* had it a ministry? *How* did we relate what we were doing to the name of Jesus Christ and his gospel? After one meeting of the Theological Commission I came away completely discouraged because one of the prominent members (who seemed to have the confidence of our leaders) announced that we need not bother any more with the ecumenical movement because "the ecumenical movement has shot its bolt." After that meeting I remember encountering at the airport a Connecticut minister who was a member of the Worship Commission, and who was coming away from his meeting similarly discouraged. I said that I thought the time had come for me to resign, and he responded, "Stick with it because we must work to bring about a change."

I stuck with it, but there were not many signs of encouragement. Then, at what turned out to be the last meeting of that commission, a new member said, "I think we should go round this table and ask what each member thinks should be the basic task of this commission." When it came to my turn I said, "I am going to say what I said at the very first meeting of this commission: we should help our churches to understand their essential nature and purpose by studying the nature of the church and its ministry." Again it was received with considerable agreement by the members of the commission, but we were not given the opportunity to do much about it because in the next series of budget cuts, the Theological Commission disappeared, and as far as I know, no one made as much as a murmur. I do know that not even a letter of explanation was sent to its members.

That was theologically irresponsible, and it has made for division rather than unity because with the failure to work out a genuinely ecumenical theological basis for the United Church of Christ, our constituent members and ministers inevitably go back to such theology as they can find in their own individual theological traditions. Either that, or we assume a purely pragmatic view of the church: a political institution to sanctify what we have, on the basis of our social or political prejudices, which means that we have already decided what should be our social and political goals without any reference to theological authorities.

THE UCC CONSTITUTION AND BYLAWS

Perhaps in the Providence of God we are better off than we deserve to be, for the *Constitution and Bylaws* do reflect a theology of the church, although, to my knowledge, it has never been set down in a systematic form. The most explicit theology appears in the Preamble, where we assert (a) the oneness of the church, (b) the need for Christian witness to be made in unity, (c) the supreme headship of Jesus Christ for his church, and (d) our acknowledgment that the church is not limited to ourselves, but is a fellowship in Christ of "all who share in this confession."[2]

The Preamble

It is clear from the Preamble that, while acknowledging the basic importance of the traditional authorities, we no longer appeal to any one of them exclusively, but see them rather as supporting and confluent testimonies to what our Lord wants his church to be and to do. So we declare that the UCC

looks to the Word of God in the Scriptures, and to the presence and power of the Holy Spirit, to prosper its creative and redemptive work in the world. It claims as its own the faith of the historic Church expressed in the ancient creeds and reclaimed in the basic insights of the Protestant Reformation.[3]

This is a clear statement about where we should stand in relation to Christian doctrine: the truths of scripture speaking of God's Word to us, understood in faith that the same Holy Spirit will reveal that living Word to us, also find their testimony in the historical creeds and in the insights of the Reformers.

But this revelation is never static; the Christ who is "the same yesterday, today and for ever" has to be constantly reinterpreted in terms that can be understood by each successive generation. So the Church (UCC)

affirms the responsibility of the Church to each generation to make this faith its own in reality of worship, in honesty of thought and expression, and in purity of heart before God. In accordance with the teaching of our Lord and the practice prevailing among evangelical Christians, it recognizes two sacraments: Baptism and the Lord's Supper or Holy Communion.[4]

This section is important in its affirmation of the continuous work of the Spirit in guiding the church, not so much into new truth in the sense of a new and different revelation, but into new insights about the one revelation of God given to us in Jesus Christ. If that part of the section is not seen in direct relationship with the earlier words in the section about scripture and the ancient creeds, then it could easily degenerate into simple humanism or theological "with-it-ness." It was, I believe, the intention of those who framed the Preamble that this should not be so; it must be equally obvious that in the minds of many members that has happened.

But the vagueness of our ecclesiology in relation to our polity and government comes out in #3:

The provisions herein define and regulate the General Synod and those Instrumentalities of the United Church of Christ which are recognized, established by or responsible to the General Synod, and describe the free and voluntary relationships which the local churches, Associations, Conferences and ministers sustain with the General Synod and with each other. The pattern of relationships and procedures so described is recommended to local churches, Associations, Conferences and ministers, to enable them more effectively to accomplish their tasks and the work of the United Church of Christ.[5]

Four sets of ecclesiastical relationships are recognized:

1. The General Synod and the Instrumentalities that are established by it and/or are directly responsible to it. That relationship *appears* to be one in which the Instrumentalities depend on General Synod.
2. Local congregations, associations, conferences, and (by implication) the General Synod itself. This much more lateral relationship is basic to our ecclesiology because each component is an expression of the church itself and not (as an Instrumentality is) of a *part* of the church, a special interest in one part of the church's work. Some would say, of course, that in not arranging these corporate expressions of our churchmanship in a hierarchical form, we are simply illustrating the vagueness of our own ecclesiology; but seen in its best light, and in the light of some aspects of our history, it *ought* to be seen as an expression of mutual ministry—a spiritual dialogue in which all the elements engage as equals before God and in which each should be ready to listen and learn.
3. Local congregations to the Instrumentalities, which seems to be through the relationship that each has to General Synod.
4. Finally, any idea of force being used in any of these relationships is explicitly excluded when the Preamble states that "the pattern of relationships and procedures so described is *recommended* to local churches, Associations, Conferences and ministers" to help them to fulfill their mission and the mission of the church.

Now this is clearly not the classic form of presbyterian polity, for there is no hierarchical system of church courts arranged in ascending authority for the sake of good order, but equally it is not the classic form of congregationalism, in which the synod had distinct authority for the clarification and definition of doctrine, and which knew nothing of "Instrumentalities."

Therefore, if these Instrumentalities are to be regarded as *necessary* for the fulfillment of the church's purpose in world mission, in home evangelism, in providing for the ministry, in winning social justice (to cite but a few of the responsibilities they cover), then it should be clear that our actual ecclesiology goes well beyond what was provided for in the traditional polities, presbyterial or congregational. In Article IV. 7 we declare that both Evangelical and Reformed and Congregational Christian churches have united "without break in their respective historic continuities and traditions," but that must be understood as representing a dynamic, living tradition: it is not simply an assertion that we reproduce the patterns of the past.

The Articles on the Church

When one looks at the Articles of the Constitution that deal with the Church, one is immediately struck by the progression of thought. We start with the grass roots as the primary expression of the church (Article IV), then to its ministry (Article V), then to its corporate expressions in Associations and Conferences (Article VI) and in the General Synod (Article VII), and end with the Instrumentalities that these corporate expressions of mission and ministry have caused us to call into being (Article VIII). There is a clear ecclesiology implied here that arises directly from the several traditions that constitute the UCC, for we are declaring, in effect, that although the primary, atomic form of the church is the local covenanted community, if that local community of Christians is to engage in the church's mission effectively, it will be in community with others.

It is true that a good deal of space in Article IV is taken up with defining and safeguarding the "autonomy of the local church" because the emphases of the older Puritan Congregationalists in this regard were filtered through the nineteenth century. It is remarkable to me that this particular provision, which was necessary in order to disabuse some of our brethren of any curtailment of their "traditional" privileges by the union, is entirely concerned with the rights of the local community to manage its own affairs and to control such matters as its own funds, but it does not attempt to clarify the spiritual authority on which the claims are based. The Puritan forebears of congregationalism would have been horrified, and I think rightly so, for if autonomy or any other power is to be asserted in the church as a right, it can be justified only by being placed on a proper theological base. We are not our own to do as we please, nor are we simply democrats reflecting post-Jeffersonian democracy; we are people under the claims of Christ.

Article XIV reflects a better understanding of the spirit of the church, when it speaks of the relationship between local congregations and the rest of the fellowship. The statement that "in mutual Christian concern and in dedication to Jesus Christ, the head of the Church, the one and the many share in common Christian experience and responsibility" expresses the principle of mutual ministry. This is the basic principle that ought to safeguard local church autonomy and define its parameters. In the best insights of both the classic Reformed and Congregational traditions, the final expression of the church of Jesus Christ is not independence, but *interdependence*. In the final issue, in a situation of persecution or enforced separation, the Church Catholic may be expressed by the local church community, but that is the extreme case, and in normal circumstances a church community that rejects the fellowship of others, or that insists on its own separation from the rest of the family, has become sectarian and schismatic: Christians need one another.

From this point of view I would like to see Article IV. 16 strengthened in two ways. First, pronouncements that come from General Synod, conferences, and associations should be taken with the highest seriousness (and not simply held in high regard) by local churches, but second, only *as they are seen to be consistent with the Word of God*. Pronouncements that are simply the expression of a political majority's will on a given day may very properly be withstood by the local church. However, our churches and ministers should be encouraged to think theologically, to examine such pronouncements according to an instructed understanding of God's Word. Pronouncements that come to us with the weight of the gospel behind them should carry the authority of the gospel to us. Our ecclesiology should encourage both associations and agencies to cast their pronouncements in those terms, and our local churches should examine such pronouncements for such terms. If the response is weak from local churches, perhaps it is because pronouncements by the "church" on any other basis are irrelevant.

There is little in respect to Articles VI, VII, and VIII that needs comment at this stage, except two things that are important for our ecclesiology:

1. In stressing the essential relationship of the minister to an association, and the association as the body that "determines, confers, and certifies to ministerial standing in the U.C.C.," we have affirmed the important principle that a minister has responsibility *as*

a minister to the wider church, and not simply to his or her own congregation. This modifies and expands the ministry in a way that is surely in line with the New Testament, and it gets rid of any temptation to affirm an atomistic view of independency. If a minister has a major responsibility to the *gospel,* that must be a responsibility that is carried to the local church for what P.T. Forsyth called "the Great Church."

2. Although we have insisted on maintaining the autonomy of associations, conferences, and the General Synod, we put this on the wrong basis when this is simply seen in terms of autonomy. Surely the positive principle involved here is not autonomy, but mutuality: we carry mutual responsibility in ministry to one another. The freedom of our corporate expressions of the church is grounded not in their independence, but in their interdependence and mutual ministry toward one another.

CRITIQUE AND QUESTIONS

Some criticisms and questions arise when we look at the *Constitution and Bylaws* as a whole, and they underline our need to undergird what we are doing in the church with an adequate theology of the church.

1. Little is said about the idea of covenant that has been at the heart of so much in our Reformed history. We speak of the covenant relationship between a minister and his or her local congregation (V. 24), but surely the covenant idea is at the heart of all our ecclesial relationships.

It is strange that this theological insight, which has played such an important part in our own heritage, should receive such slight attention, and it may be that this prevents us from making the kind of contribution we could be making ecumenically. (It is worth noting that COCU is now paying serious attention to that idea as the biblical concept that may very well aid the further unity of the churches in the immediate future.[6])

2. It is strange that we say so little about the spiritual qualifications we expect to find in those who are called to exercise leadership in our church. We are careful to lay down precise rules about the

proper proportion of laity, ministers, women, minorities, young people to be appointed to our church committees, and this is good. But we are not a purely political or social organization. Are we ashamed to say that we are also looking for those who are outstanding for their gifts of the Spirit, or have we become so secularized that these matters are no longer relevant? Perhaps we can assume them . . . ? Are we anxious simply to have a point of view represented, or are we concerned to have that point of view represented *in the name of the gospel and in the spirit of reconciliation?*

3. Should we not say more than we do about the Conference Minister? Is he/she simply to be regarded as an executive of the conference, or is not he or she called especially to exercise leadership in a ministry to the ministry? We may have valid historic reasons for turning away from the term bishop, but with all their faults I doubt whether the Catholic branches of the church would define their concept of "bishop" in the purely administrative and executive terms we have used.

We have a much better concept of what it ought to mean to be a "minister to ministers," or a representative of the wider church family to a congregation in need of love and concern. Why are we afraid to say so, and to explain what we expect a Conference Minister to be?

Whether we are aware of it or not, there is a *tacit* theology of the church that the *Constitution and Bylaws* present, and a good deal of it is based on pragmatism. But pragmatism is not to be brushed aside as irrelevant to the gospel, and I have argued elsewhere that it has its proper place in ecclesiology.[7] But is the priority of the pragmatic the major impression that we wish to leave for our view of the church? The time has come for a systematic approach to our theology of the church, not on the basis of exclusive adherence to past ecclesiologies—although we should be aware of them and recognize the truths they tried to enshrine—but on the basis of our fundamental mission and ministry. For ultimately if the church points to God by its very nature, then what we need is a *theology* of the church, that is, a concept of the church that is related directly to what we proclaim about God and God's love for the world in Jesus Christ.

Chapter 6
The Doctrine of the
Church (I)

If I were responsible for teaching the course on polity in our seminaries, I would insist that the subject be taught as part of a course on the doctrine of the church. For the question of how the church is governed and what polity it uses is *secondary;* it is not important in itself except as it is seen to arise out of the church's essential nature. To give it the kind of importance it has assumed in the past is to suggest that the mission of the church is defined by its form, whereas, in my understanding of the New Testament, the form was dictated by the church's nature and mission. Form is *important,* but only as an instrument of the gospel, not as that which conditions or controls the gospel.

So I turn now to the problem of defining the doctrine of the church. What can be said about the church's essential nature and mission, and how *does* this affect the shape that it should assume in the world? This is our basic issue, although it should be clear that before anything useful can be said about our ecclesiology in the future, the fundamental authority on which such an ecclesiology should be based must be established.

AUTHORITY AGAIN

The three major approaches to the doctrine of the church that served churches in times past cannot be appealed to exclusively. And let it be admitted that these approaches are open to fundamental question because of pressures that spring directly from the historical, scientific, and social revolutions of the past century. From that perspective we must also admit that, insofar as they are concerned with *truth,* the "secular" challenges that have come from our age must be seen not as working against the gospel of Jesus Christ, but as forcing Christians to take their gospel more seriously.[1] God has been using similar forces to strip the church of its prejudiced mythologies—and there is nothing we have been willing to clothe with more archaic mythology than our favorite brand of church government.

For example, the forms of the church that based their authority on the way the church itself had developed are under question, not so much because historical succession itself is questionable, but because those who established their own control of the church have not given evidence of the "fruits of the Spirit" that are the authentic marks of the church of Jesus Christ. So the rejection of the church at this point by our contemporaries (whether they recognize it or not) is centered *in* the gospel. When secular people see the evidence of church leaders basing their claims on forged credentials, or using the persuasion of prison, fire, and sword to assert their authority, or maintaining their own wealth while neglecting the poor and dispossessed, then the *secular* criticism has to be seen as made in the name of Jesus Christ, whether it is made by a Marxist, a person of another religion, or a person of no religion.

Similarly, biblical restorationism has to be questioned in its literal forms, not so much because it is too literally bound to the pattern of the church in scripture, but because this scriptural appeal is seen to be built on false assumptions about the Bible, and because the actual dividedness of the church has arisen from sincerely held misinterpretations of scripture in a way that visibly denies the unity of the Spirit that was to have been a basic testimony to the Holy Spirit's presence in the church. When African animists, Asian Buddhists, Arab Muslims, or European Marxists see the actual rivalry of Christian missions, or witness the warfare carried on between so-called Christian nations, or note their silence in the face of other people's poverty and suffering, then—whatever the actual name in which they voice their criticism—they are voicing it *in the name of Jesus Christ.*

So, too, we have to criticize the adequacy of spiritual pragmatics as an exclusive and sufficient basis for ecclesiology, not because of its emphasis on attainable practical objectives for the church, but because it so often confuses the goals of pure pragmatism with those of the practicality that *serves* the gospel of Christ. What is the black city laborer or the poor white in a rural area to think when he or she witnesses the church (at the command of some distant central agency or board) pull up its roots in the central city or in a depressed village, where it could exercise an indispensable but sacrificial ministry, to relocate in some already well-endowed suburb? Or when more emphasis seems to be placed on the church's material plant and physical property than on its own God-given mission of witness and service? The criticism such a disillusionment voices is expressed *in the name of Christ*. We must take it seriously, for when the secular world utters such criticisms of the church for its false claims, its presumptions, its insensitivity, and its apostasy, it may well be the voice of God.

But before we leave this rejection of the former authorities by which the churches in the past justified their own "rightness," we should note that the arrogance we are criticizing came about because each of these authorities regarded itself as the *exclusive* authority to which a particular church appealed in order to justify itself. Exclusiveness produces arrogance. A very different attitude comes about when we see them not as *exclusive* channels of the Holy Spirit, but as *complementary* channels of grace—when, for example, the appeal to the church of the New Testament is seen in relationship to the changing needs of a historical development, and when both what the church was and what it has become are also brought into direct relationship to the practical needs of our mission today. Then we see that we are not presented with an infallible blueprint to last throughout all time unchanged, but we are given three testimonies of the Holy Spirit that all point toward Jesus Christ and that invite us to discover his will for the church by walking forward confidently in faith.

A BIBLICAL THEOLOGY
OF THE CHURCH

The holistic way to see the problem of authority beneath our search for a truly ecumenical ecclesiology is through a biblical theology of the church, but can we clarify it further? What are we to say about that emphasis on the biblical testimony that is so much at the heart of what our component UCC traditions have maintained in matters of churchmanship?

First, among the three ecclesiological testimonies to which we have referred, a proper priority has to be given to the scriptural evidence, not because we are anxious to extrapolate every little detail of New Testament church practice and reinstate it in twentieth-century America, but because our faith has its birth in historical events, and the Bible remains the basic historical record. Most ministers and members will not regard that record in the sacrosanct way it was understood in the past, but if it contains the Word of God to us, we had better not treat it as irrelevant. Indeed, unless it does contain God's living Word to us, it is difficult to see what gospel—"good news"—we can possibly have for this or any other age.

But how are we to find the scriptural basis for that gospel in relationship to the church? Is there any biblical basis for ecclesiology that will give us, at one and the same time, both the assurance that we are grounded in the Word of God, Jesus Christ, and the flexibility that he promised the church in his Spirit, to interpret anew that gospel for succeeding ages? Any such basis for church and ministry must be firmly grounded in the biblical revelation because we must remember that we are not just talking about any society, nor even about any *religious* society, but we are speaking about the church of Jesus Christ; yet whatever that revelation declares must center in Christ and his message, rather than in the details of church administration followed by the apostolic church. The apostles adopted certain practices in the church (and they were by no means uniform practices) *so that the church could make its testimony and engage in its mission effectively* to that society and at that time. This is a distinction in biblical interpretation that we must make if we are to avoid falling into stultifying literalism, legalism, or rationalism.

The only valid starting place is in the *theology* of the Bible. I would like to have said that the only valid starting place is a "biblical theology," but this term has had so many negative connotations in recent years, being equated with the kind of neo-literalism that was often associated with the later stages of the neoorthodox movement of the 1940s and 1950s. This is unfortunate because we may have to get back to some of the better insights of that movement without falling into the trap of allowing our appeal to the scriptural revelation to jockey us into new forms of literalism. But whether we call the method the "theology of the Bible" or "biblical theology," what we are concerned with is *what the Bible has to say about God,* what it has to say about the divine nature as it was revealed in Jesus Christ, what it has to say about God's relationships with God's people, and what it has to say about God's relationships through Christ and Christians to the rest of creation.

There is a distinction to be made between doctrine and theology. Doctrine is the systematization of our theology in regard to special issues, but *theology* is essentially what we believe about God. The "theology of the Bible" is therefore what the Bible reveals to us about God. And this is the starting place because no doctrine is of any significance if it does not have that as its central point of reference. At the center of this biblical revelation there is the revelation of God's nature and the divine will for us in Jesus Christ— Christology—to which the scriptures testified first, but to which the historic church has witnessed from the time of the apostles, and to which testimonies of the Spirit, the Holy Spirit in our own hearts add their own "Amen!"

Therefore, a theology of the church (or ecclesiology), if it is to produce a valid doctrine of the church for us, must point back to Jesus Christ and to his relationship with the One he called "Father," just as any valid doctrine of Ministry must go back to *his* ministry and to the life begun in the Incarnation. Any valid doctrine of the church must point back explicitly to the relationships that Christ expressed toward God and God's people. In the church we are concerned with a people who are in pilgrimage toward becoming the true people *of such a God*. A truly biblical theology of the church will not claim that the church has already arrived at that point (except possibly in the eyes of God, although that is something on which it is better not to speculate), for that has been the mistake of all the ecclesiologies that have claimed their own version of the church to be already perfect, impeccable, and sacrosanct. At the same time a biblical theology of the church will recognize, first, that the church is called to point to the divine nature of God, and second, that on this earth it is always in pilgrimage toward that goal.

If there is one point where we should use Bunyan to correct Bonhoeffer it is perhaps here, for Bunyan always recognized that we have not yet fully arrived, whereas in Bonhoeffer's concept of the "world come of age" there is at least the suggestion that we may have gotten there already. But unless we can state with perfect assurance that the *eschaton* has already arrived in its fullness, and that we have reached perfection both as Christian individuals and as churches, we need to keep before us that fact that we are in pilgrimage—very much in the spirit of Paul, who admitted "not that I have already obtained this or am already perfect; but I press on to make it my own, because Christ Jesus has made me his own [Phil. 3:12]."

An ecclesiology that is based on biblical theology will try to show in terms of organization, ministry, and service what is the nature of the people *of God,* the people *of such a God.* It will in that way be biblically *based* but not biblically *bound* in the sense of trying to tie the church of the twentieth and twenty-first centuries to the details of church practice appropriate in the first century A.D. It will be less concerned with discovering proof texts to justify practices adopted in the time of Peter or Paul than with recognizing how appropriate those practices were for the church's witness at that time, and then asking how the church of our own day can be equally faithful in its own time. Instead of going to the scriptures to mine textual rocks to throw at the Episcopalians and the Roman Catholics, with an occasional side heave at the Baptists and the Methodists, we now have to ask what the Bible has to say about God and God's people. *How can we show ourselves corporately to be the people of such a God?*

The old arguments whether episcopacy, presbyterianism, or congregationalism can be proved from the church of the New Testament are now seen to be irrelevant; nor does it make any further sense to try to prove legalistically our apostolic blue blood through one ecclesiastical family tree rather than another: the very bases on which our ancestors ground out their apologetic are not only questionable in the name of historical truth, but they have been invalidated by the unethical means we have used to establish our understanding of the truth in our dealings with one another. If the church points to God in Christ, ethics can never be divorced from ecclesiology.

THE PATTERN OF A BIBLICAL ECCLESIOLOGY

What is implied about the church by our theology? How does what we believe about God assist us in developing a firmer basis for our own ecclesiology? This is something on which one person cannot hope to exhaust all the possibilities and implications, but here are a few.

God's concern is universal. God is concerned with all humankind, and we cannot represent anything more limited than that universal concern as the concern of the church. "God so loved the world"— but this has dimensions we are only just beginning to explore. It means, first, that we have to proclaim the gospel of God's love in Christ to all people without respect to nation, culture, color, age, or sex. But Paul saw further:

> For the created universe waits with eager expectation for God's sons to be revealed. It was made the victim of frustration, not by its own choice, but because of him who made it so; yet always there was hope, because the universe itself is to be freed from the shackles of mortality and enter upon the liberty and splendour of the children of God. Up to the present, we know, the whole created universe groans in all its parts as if in the pangs of childbirth. Not only so, but even we, to whom the Spirit is given as firstfruits of the harvest to come, are groaning inwardly while we wait for God to make us his sons and set our whole body free. (Rom. 8:19–23, NEB)

This must mean that there is a sense in which the church is involved in the redemption of God's *whole* creation. The ecology issue, the question of endangered species, the yearly slaughter with which we often celebrate festivals of Christmas and Thanksgiving may not be the primary targets of the church's mission, but they cannot be excluded from our concern.

God works through the Holy Spirit. We should learn from the pentecostalists that the gift of the Holy Spirit to the church lies at the center of the New Testament's testimony. There is no need to interpret that gift in any narrow way, but it surely means that God is willing to use many different means and to employ many kinds of people in order to achieve the divine purposes. If God can use Nebuchadnezzar, Cyrus, and Darius, the kings of Persia, it is a fairly clear indication that however inflexible God may be in the divine purposes, God has an extremely flexible attitude about the means used to achieve those ends.

And so, too, with the church. The great danger that we see illustrated in the history of the church is that practically every church has understood itself in fixed and unchangeable terms that have prevented it from adapting to meet the needs of its own time. The list is obvious; the New Testament church, the Protestant churches, Puritanism, Methodism, the Salvation Army, and a host of other groups arose largely because religious people of their time were not flexible enough to meet the evangelistic needs of that age.[2] The churches were often so captivated by the unchangeableness of God that they did not see the divine willingness to be flexible for the sake of an unchangeable purpose, and hence they cast the community of God's people in fixed and unchangeable terms. A doctrine of the Holy Spirit means that we have to insist that God retains the freedom to adapt the church's form and methods to the needs of the gospel in each succeeding age.

The principle of incarnation is not only at the center of our Christology, but must also be at the center of our ecclesiology. The church is present as God's people *in the midst of this world*. This is the opposite of the way in which often, in the name of purity, it has tried to separate itself from the world in convent or conventicle. The church testifies to the Incarnation primarily not in what it says, or even wholly in what it does, but in what it *is;* in other words, if the church does not reveal what it is by its own deeds, its presence, *and its own form,* it invalidates anything it says about the incarnation in its preaching and official pronouncements.

Christ's incarnation was for the purpose of redemption. Incarnation is for the purpose of redemption. This qualifies the way in which the idea of incarnation can be applied to the church. Too often the idea of incarnation has been applied to the church without that qualification, and when that has happened, there has been the temptation to consider the church as perfect in the same way that Christ was perfect. It can lead to ecclesiolatry—the self-worship of the church.

The church is "perfect" only as it exists to bring about the redemption of the world. Its perfection is like that of Jesus' own body. It was not perfect in the sense that it could not die, could not feel pain, or was not subject to the needs of a physical body; it was "perfect" only in the sense that it was the perfect vehicle of redemption. Much the same is true of the church, its "perfection"—seen only by God—is only as it becomes the agent of salvation for which it was called. It exists to fulfill God's purpose for it and in it. Any claim to perfection or infallibility as a *right* that it carries within itself goes further than Jesus himself was prepared to go. Jesus made no claims for himself and was unwilling for others to make them for him. In no less than three of his recorded miracles he charged those involved to tell nobody,[3] and he said the same to Peter after his great affirmation at Caesarea Philippi (Mark 8:30; Matthew 16:20; Luke 9:21). He remonstrated with the rich young ruler, "Why do you ask me about what is good? One there is who is good [Matt. 19:17]." He was content to do what he did and be what he was, and then he left people to draw their own conclusions, but he made no claims for himself.

Telling people would not do any good. There was a time when the rulers and others asked him to tell them plainly whether he was the Christ, but he answered, "If I tell you, you will not believe [Luke 22:67]." The proof was in the deed, and in his person—that is, not in isolated deeds, but in the consistent living out of his redemptive mission. There was another occasion, relatively early in his ministry, when John the Baptist sent to him asking him much the same question.

> John, who was in prison, heard what Christ was doing, and sent his own disciples to him with this message: "Are you the one who is to come, or are we to expect some other?" Jesus answered, "Go and tell John what you hear and see: the blind recover their sight, the lame walk, the lepers are made clean, the deaf hear, the dead are raised to life, the poor are hearing the good news—and happy is the man who does not find me a stumbling-block. (Matt. 11:2–6, NEB)

Jesus let the deeds speak for themselves, and how much more this should be true for the church.

God's purpose to humankind is reconciliation. The apostle Paul saw this with great clarity, but notice, in the following passage, how God's reconciliation of us to himself in Christ is carried on in the ministry and mission of the church.

> From first to last this has been the work of God. He has reconciled us men [people] to himself through Christ, and he has enlisted us in this service of reconciliation. What I mean is, that God was in Christ reconciling the world to himself, no longer holding men's misdeeds against them, and that he has entrusted us with the message of reconciliation. We come therefore as Christ's ambassadors. It is as if God were appealing to you through us: in Christ's name, we implore you, be reconciled to God! Christ was innocent of sin, and yet for our sake God made him one with the sinfulness of men, so that in him we might be made one with the goodness of God himself. Sharing in God's work, we urge this appeal upon you. (2 Cor. 5:18—6:1, NEB; cf. Rom. 5:10)

This is where the mission starts, in the good news of reconciliation with God, and perhaps we have to remind our church that that is the center. But this is simply the beginning, as the implications of the reconciliation are worked out in the relationship of nation to nation, culture to culture, race to race, man to woman, youth to age, human being to the rest of the creation, person to the self. And high on that list is the task of reconciliation that still needs to be done in the church—our ecumenical mission that involves not only the relationship of denomination to denomination and Protestant to Catholic, but also the possibly more intractable ones of liberal to conservative and social activist to evangelical. This is where commitment to Christ's reconciling word will be tested most severely.

Christ the servant. It is doubtful whether even the New Testament writers ever consciously thought of *God* as a serving God, but that is where their experience of Jesus Christ points. As Paul says:

> Let your bearing towards one another arise out of your life in Christ Jesus. For the divine nature was his from the first; yet he did not think to snatch at equality with God, but made himself nothing, assuming the nature of a slave. Bearing the human likeness, revealed in human shape, he humbled himself, and in obedience accepted even death—death on a cross. *Therefore* God raised him to the heights and bestowed on him the name above all names, that at the name of Jesus every knee should bow—in heaven, on earth, and in the depths—and every tongue confess, "Jesus Christ is Lord," to the glory of God the Father. (Phil. 2:5–11, NEB)

(The glorification of Christ is directly *because of* his servanthood. This indicates that the only possible ground for a triumphal view of the church is not in its *claim* to glory, but precisely in its *refusal* to claim glory.)

In this passage Paul recognized the *essential* servanthood of Jesus, and we have the same insight in the words of Jesus himself when his disciples had been arguing which of them should be first in the kingdom of God and he declared: "Among you, whoever wants to be great must be your servant, and whoever would be first must be the willing slave of all—like the Son of Man; he did not come to be served, but to serve, and to give up his life as a ransom for many [Matt. 20:28, NEB]."

The serving nature of God in Christ points directly to the serving nature of the Christian community: we are called to *leadership in service,* and if our ecclesiology has its grounding in the place we have suggested, it means that our church should be so organized that it makes that clear both to its own members and to the rest of the world. One Christian organization has changed the name of what used to be called its "headquarters" to "International Service Center," and that seems a move in the right direction. In the final analysis, however, what we demonstrate about the way we govern ourselves will be indicated less by nomenclature than by the *spirit* that pervades our administrative agencies.

Christ in community. There is one thing that the church is able to do in Christ's name that Jesus could not do in his own person, and that is to translate the meaning of his servanthood into terms of a human community. I tried to point this out in *The Church in Search of Its Self:*

> The Church has one distinctive element in relation to ministry that is its own. That is its corporateness, for in the Church the meaning of our Lord's ministry is translated into terms of an ongoing, living *community.* The Church is therefore an essential link between our Lord's ministry and the realization of the Kingdom, for the Kingdom of God cannot be realized until it can be demonstrated that what Jesus brought to men can produce this kind of new community: the *koinonia* of the New Testament Church is the love of Jesus Christ expressed in community.
>
> This is the unique significance of the Church. Throughout church history we seem to have veered between emphasis on the corporateness of the Church and an emphasis on the election of its individual members. The one tended to deify the Church's unity but lost the commitment of the individual, whereas the other maintained individual commitment at the expense of the corporate unity. The significance of the Church is that it is called to be both holy and united. . . . On the other hand, the Church is not simply an aggregate of Christians, however committed or however holy. It is a *community* which has been called into covenant with God, and in which the members find themselves in covenant with one another.[4]

There are two aspects of our ecclesiology that we have to take with new seriousness. On the one hand, we do have to challenge our members with the need for their own personal commitment, at a level somewhat deeper than is demanded by membership in the local country club. But we have to take the *corporate* nature of the church with as deep a commitment, for if the church points to the reign of God, it is the church in its corporate capacity that is the evangelizing agent in the world.

We need to recast the theology of evangelism to include the necessary testimony of the church as a community. It has been expounded too exclusively in individualist terms. The individual aspect is important—indeed it is an indispensable aspect of evangelism. The Roman Catholic Church has begun to realize the vital function of individual lay Christians as evangelists. Shortly after Vatican II, lay Catholics met in various meetings throughout the United States to learn skills in evangelism. Nearly 5,000 persons gathered on one of these occasions at the Civic Center in Hartford, Connecticut. With declining numbers of priests and the possibility of revival in the churches, one of the leaders at the meeting concluded that "lay people will have to do much of the work now performed by priests." In many churches in Latin America that is already the case, and it often proves to be "a blessing in disguise" because of the way laity become involved in the life of the church and experience a renewed vitality in their own faith.[5]

There are then these two aspects of ecclesiology that have to be taken with new seriousness. First, we have to challenge members with the need for personal commitment and witness at a deeper level. This involves the personal testimony of lay Christians. I am reminded of a comment made by Bishop Stephen Neill while he was giving a report on evangelism at the Amsterdam Assembly of the World Council of Churches in 1948, when he pointed out how unthinkable it would be for any industrial firm to limit productivity to about only 5 percent of its work force; but that this was precisely what the churches did when they relied only on their ordained ministry to be responsible for evangelism. Perhaps the comment has even more force among Western churches now that we have become more conscious that we live in, if not a completely secularized society, at least a society in which a majority of the citizens live perfectly contentedly without the church and the gospel.

Second, and perhaps more important, we have to take the *corporate* nature of the church with new seriousness, for if the church points to the reign of God, it is the church in its corporate entity that is the primary evangelizing agent to human societies. Certainly the gospel is concerned with the salvation of individuals, but it is also concerned with announcing that God embraces the whole of human society. A theology of evangelism has to involve a theology of the church. It is true that there is no explicit statement of the doctrine of the Trinity in the Bible, but it is also clear that as the New Testament writers wrestled with their experience of God—in the Old Testament writings, in the life of Jesus, and in the Holy Spirit within the church—this inevitably produced a view of the Triune Godhead: The doctrine of the Trinity represents a Godhead in which relationships are recognized and are primary. Which aspects of God are active in our redemption?—Obviously Jesus, the one whom God acknowledged as Son, but also "God the Father," who initiated the Incarnation as the divine Word and Will, and also the Holy Spirit, whose special function was to reveal the truth of Christ to the Church.[6] All parts of the Godhead are involved, and this suggests that God may be thought of Christianly as a *community* of relationships. I would maintain that the church has described that in terms of the Trinity, not because this provides us with an accurate and definitive formula of Godhead, but because God is *at least* this. If community is to be understood so profoundly at the heart of what we believe, then it is clear that the communal aspects of the people of God are an essential part of the church's witness. Our churches may need to produce evangelists, but perhaps it is even more important that our churches need to be communal evangelists. As P.T. Forsyth declared in 1913, "The greatest truth is given and promised to a Church. The Apostle to Society is a Society."[7] This is where our evangelism needs to place its distinctive emphasis: to show itself the redemptive community that proclaims the gospel in word and action to human society.

Chapter 7
The Doctrine of the
Church (II)

In the preceding major division of our subject I concentrated on the universality of God's purpose, but now I must turn to the opposite side of the coin and recognize that God achieves that purpose by selecting particular people. We cannot ignore the principle of special choice and "Election" that runs through the whole of the Bible in its account of *Heilsgeschichte,* the story of salvation. The choice of Adam, the choice of Noah, the choice of Abraham, the choice of Israel, the choice of Moses, Joshua, and David; the choice of the prophets to a chosen people. Nor can we ignore the choice of Eve, of Sarah, of Tamar, Rahab, and Ruth in the genealogy of Jesus; the choice of Mary. The final example is the "choice" of Jesus himself (cf. Mark 1:10–11). God's purpose is universal, but God chooses those who can best enter into this purpose and further that intention.

THE DANGERS OF ELECTION

There are obvious dangers when the idea of a Chosen People or of Election is divorced from the universality of God's purpose. Christians have always justified themselves by claiming to be God's specially chosen people while perpetrating cruelty against others. No heresiarch or bloodthirsty apocalyptic prophet has ever arisen who did not claim that he (and very occasionally she) had been specially called by God to fulfill this destiny. The sense of being a chosen people was used to justify Britain's imperial empire in Africa, America's claim to "Manifest Destiny," the idea of the "White Man's burden," and the superiority of the Anglo-Saxon peoples.

There was a curious fusion between these religious ideas of special election that came from traditional Protestantism and the new science of biology in the nineteenth century. When religious convictions about being a chosen people appeared to be given scientific support by doctrines of "the struggle for existence" and "the survival of the fittest," this gave rise to a ruthless expansion into Africa and the Pacific by the nations of Europe and the West. One historian has observed:

> The tone of realism, not to say ruthlessness and brutality, that was so striking a characteristic of imperialism was due in a measure to the general cast of sociological thought prevailing at that time. A large number of contemporary writers remarked on the tremendous vogue of Darwinian theories of social evolution. The phrases *struggle for existence* and *survival of the fittest* carried everything before them in the nineties.[1]

There is a real irony that it was the confluence of a secularized doctrine of special Election and Darwin's theory of the survival of the fittest that led to the remarkable expansion of imperialism in the late nineteenth century, and it has been pointed out that this "social Darwinism" had the twofold effect of producing the militarism that led to World War I, and the ideas of racial superiority and of a divine national mission.[2]

It is questionable whether either Darwinism alone or the doctrine of Election alone would have had that dramatic effect. It is fascinating to see how the former secularized the latter, and if anyone is tempted to think that this imperialistic climate of violent competition and its justification in success could be held only by the secular elements in society, or the peoples of decadent Europe, let them reflect on those Americans of simple faith and fundamentalist propensities who have no difficulty in applying these principles to their business practices or in the pursuit of denominational competition. But a secularized doctrine of Election, as we see it in the idea of a "Chosen People" in communism or in Hitler's idea of the *Herrenvolk,* can be devastating. As in so many areas of life, the corruption of the best can become the worst.

Perhaps, however, the world has less to fear from the aberrations of a *secularized* doctrine of Special Choice and Election than from the abuse and misapplication of the doctrine by the church itself, for constantly churches have claimed, as of right, the glory that Jesus received from God only after the resurrection. I would remind you of the passage quoted earlier (Philippians 2:5–11); *because* Christ was content to become a slave and humbled himself, God has "raised him to the heights and bestowed on him the name above all names, that at the name of Jesus every knee should bow . . . and every tongue confess, "Jesus Christ is Lord," to the glory of God the Father." But churches have forgotten the first part in their anxiety to claim the second, just as Christian individuals can sometimes give a totally wrong impression of what the gospel is about by oozing arrogance and the smugness of being "saved." Saved from what? Certainly not from the sin of smugness and arrogance. The world is rightly nauseated, just as the world turns away from churches when they claim the glory and status of spiritual imperialism in the name of the One who was content to become a servant and who wore a crown of thorns.

And yet we cannot erase from the Bible, or from the relationships between God and human beings that are recorded in the Bible, the clear testimony that when God has something special to be done, God takes pains to select the right persons for the task. And where a community is needed in order to give that a corporate expression, God chooses a particular community—the family of Noah, the descendants of Abraham, the children of Israel, the church.

But the fundamental question we have to ask ourselves is, what are God's specially chosen people elected *for* today? We are elected to be servants—and, in the terms set by our own circumstances and history, the cross. This is the sine qua non of our election. We are elected not for incarnation in the sense of claiming to be a divine manifestation in human society, but for the purpose of *redemptive* incarnation, in which we do not claim anything of ourselves, but we may possibly *reveal* the deeds of redemption, the things that God does to redeem sinful men and women. To claim any glory about this is to invalidate the very thing that we are claiming because it is a complete contradiction of the One who did not snatch equality with God, "but made himself nothing, assuming the nature of a slave," and who, "bearing the human likeness, revealed in human shape . . . humbled himself, and in obedience accepted even death—death on a cross." Nothing could manifest a greater contradiction of the Spirit of Jesus Christ than a church that insists on its prestige and trappings, or that lives in the spirit that is "holier than thou," or that claims special privileges because it is guaranteed salvation.

The only appropriate attitude of the church and its members in regard to their election to God's special purposes is the kind of gratitude and love that devotes itself to God's service without thought of reward. I am reminded of some verses attributed to the great Jesuit missionary Francis Xavier:

> My God, I love Thee, not because
>   I hope for heaven thereby,
> Nor yet because, if I love not,
>   I must forever die.
>
> Thou, O my Jesus, Thou didst me
>   Upon the Cross embrace;
> For me didst bear the nails and spear,
>   And manifold disgrace;
>
> Then why, O blessèd Jesus Christ,
>   Should I not love Thee well?
> Not for the sake of winning heaven,
>   Or of escaping hell;
>
> Not with the hope of gaining aught,
>   Not seeking a reward;
> But as Thyself hast lovèd me,
>   O ever-loving Lord.[3]

That's it. If the church is to interpret the meaning of Christ's ministry into terms of human community, nothing less than disinterested love and obedience to God's will for the sake of the world the Creator loved into existence will do. And our *church order* must show that love and service is primary in the church's work. As far as we are concerned, our "election" is for that and that alone.

OUR COVENANT WITH GOD

We are a covenant people and the context of servanthood and service is the context within which that covenant is to be seen, lest the idea of a special relationship with God at the heart of that covenant idea should get out of hand. The sense of being in a special covenant relationship to God can become a dangerous adjunct to ecclesiastical triumphalism, racial superiority, or personal religious snobbery unless it is seen within this total biblical context. Our Lord's fate within his own nation is a clear indication of how easy it is for this to happen, even in the minds of sincerely religious people.

A good deal of interest has been aroused in the biblical idea of covenant as a paradigm for further ecumenical relationships in the churches involved in COCU.[4] Paul Crow recognized the skepticism that such an idea may receive from ministers and members in the churches who have become disillusioned with ecumenical slogans and catch phrases in the years since World War II.

A few skeptics will see covenanting proposals as just another try at an old agenda. Admittedly, it is ironic that the covenant idea is being proposed in places where earlier plans of union proved to be as yet unfruitful, e.g., New Zealand, Wales, England, South Africa, and lately the U.S.A. Yet the evidence is contrary to the skeptics' whim. Far more is represented in covenanting than an ecumenical Trojan horse. It is a profound attempt to live out, in the midst of fragmented churches, the implications of the biblical covenant between God and his people.[5]

Indeed there is some evidence on the other side. When the first attempts in the twentieth century to unite the Congregational Union of England and Wales and the Presbyterian Church of England appeared to be unsuccessful—perhaps not surprising, since they had been trying to get together unsuccessfully since the Westminster Assembly in the seventeenth century—the determination of the two denominations to keep working at it was symbolized in a solemn covenant in 1951, on which occasion Douglas Horton preached the sermon. The seriousness with which that covenant was taken is seen in the fact that in 1972, the United Reformed Church in England became reality. The incident illustrates several aspects of the biblical idea of covenant that are important for our own ecclesiastical organization and attitudes.

A covenant is initiated by God alone. One of my former colleagues, an Old Testament scholar, put it like this:

The initiative for the establishment of the agreement rests with the suzerain, not the vassal. This is self-evident, but nonetheless it is often forgotten. When we consider the Lord's covenant with Israel, it is clear that the tradition emphasizes the initiative taken by God. Israel did not seek the LORD. Rather Israel was chosen. Israel became a people and a servant at God's choosing. Israel's story began with the divine selection rather than some human action. The unexpected graciousness of this act is repeatedly emphasized by stressing Israel's complete unworthiness as an object of this Sovereign's concern.[6]

We often give lip service to this but act as if the initiative were our own, although Christians should have better insight. A moment's reflection would remind us that just as Israel's covenant had been initiated by God's saving intervention at the Red Sea, so we are only able to enter into the New Covenant because of our Lord's saving intervention in the cross.

Our covenant with God brings us into relationship with one another. But because we are brought into unique relationship with God, we are brought into a special relationship with one another. There is a passage in John Baillie's *Invitation to Pilgrimage*[7] in which he puts this graphically. He speaks of our coming to kneel at the foot of Christ's cross, and this is, of course, a personal and individual thing that we do; but when we arise we find that we have been brought into a new relationship with all those who, like ourselves, have been kneeling at that place.

The early Separatists and later Puritans extended the idea of the covenant to the relationship of members in a local church. Although we have questions about how far Robert Browne, that erratic genius of Separatism, may be regarded as responsible for later Congregational ecclesiology, he set out the principle of covenant on which their churches were based in the passage quoted earlier, and I have always been impressed with his definition of a local covenanted church.[8] As I pointed out elsewhere, this statement is very different from the voluntary societies that often did duty for "called out" churches in later Congregationalism[9]: the key to Browne's concept of the church is in the phrase "which by a willing covenant with their God." This is where all church government and ecclesiology begins; but *because it begins there,* we are brought into an integral relationship with those who share in the same covenant relationship.

Covenant is a dynamic relationship. Although the biblical covenants show God's determination of mercy toward God's chosen people, from the peoples' side it must be seen as a dynamic relationship. It is a growing relationship in which we grow into an ever deeper understanding of its implications and meaning. I like to use Christian marriage as an illustration of the distinction we have to draw between this dynamic quality in a covenant and the more static concept in a secular contract. The latter defines the legal claims of one party on the other, and that may be necessary in view of the history of marriage in our time; but unless there is a personal *covenant* between partners, marriage is on rocky ground. And this covenant relationship is one in which two persons become committed to each other because they are committed first to God—a commitment that implies a lifetime of growing together. We can see this throughout Israel's covenant relationships with God, which may be one reason why some of the most moving accounts of that relationship are cast in the pattern of a marriage relationship (e.g., Hosea; Christ and the church).

The covenant has an inclusive purpose. Although the Old Testament covenants are between Yahweh and Israel, they include the whole creation: they have an inclusive purpose. Israel is not brought into covenant relationship with God simply in order to be God's favorite among the nations, but to become a blessing to all the rest of God's peoples. This is clear from the Abramic Covenant (Genesis 12:1–3; 22:18), but the vision of universal blessing surely runs throughout the Old Testament prophets. Israel is to be a servant people in obedience to their God because they are in a covenant relationship to God. As Eugene March has said:

> Because the fact of God's selection of Israel is so prominent in the Old Testament, it is often forgotten that the LORD is also pictured as in relationship to non-Israelite people as well. The Old Testament was in the first instance directed to and preserved by Israel. Thus it was natural that Israel was the major concern and point of focus. Nonetheless, there are repeated references that indicate that some, at least, understood that the LORD was aware of and engaged with other peoples.[10]

And he cited as illustrations of this awareness Genesis 9, Amos 9, Isaiah 2, 45, 49, etc.

The problem of Israel arose eventually not because the universality of God's blessing remained unrecognized, but because the leaders of the nation were not prepared to accept that to be the chosen servants of Yahweh implied also becoming servants to those whom God was calling into the kingdom. That seemed to be carrying the business of servanthood too far.

THE COVENANT AND CHURCH ORDER

The question remains what all this has to do with the practicalities of Church Order in the UCC. I hasten to state that I have no intention of being inveigled into drawing up a comprehensive outline of what our polity should be for the next 50 or 100 years. No one person could, or should, do that; it needs the corporate wisdom and best spiritual insight of the whole church. But we can perhaps draw out a few guidelines for the consideration of government and polity in the UCC.[11]

1. It should be clear that since we recognize a somewhat different authority base from the ecclesiologies of the past, we are not *bound* to any particular polity—presbyterian, congregational, or any other. Ideally we should be free to adopt whatever form, or *forms,* of polity the gospel demands for its own effective presentation in our situation. The only limitations set on us are:

- that it should exemplify the gospel and not hinder or contradict it;
- that it should arise from the best biblical insights of our tradition into the nature of God's people;
- that it hold churches in an essential pastoral relationship: mutual ministry;
- that it hold out the hand ecumenically to other Christians;
- that it promote and exemplify service to all people and reconciliation to all God's creation;
- that, with these criteria, it be practical.

2. Our concern for freedom does not mean that order is irrelevant. Perhaps Calvin's insight (which he gained from Paul and the New Testament) is important at this point. Things should be done decently and in order: one does not witness to God by being disorganized and chaotic. There is a proper place for practicality in the church, as long as the pragmatic principle *serves* the gospel and does not pretend that practicality is an end in itself.

3. In all our government, in the way we administer our church life and resources, we have to assert the priority of *grace:* the importance of law, but the priority of grace. Somehow the Spirit of our Lord has to shine through the way we do things, in the way we treat

the errant and the dissident, in the compassion we show to people, in the conservation and care we exercise in regard to things, and in the way we treat all God's creation. Law *is* important, but in the final issue the supreme law is the law of mercy and of grace. Richard Baxter observed that he disliked some Puritans in the seventeenth century because "they were not tender enough to dissenting Brethren, but too much *against Liberty* as others were too much *for it;* and thought by Votes and Numbers to do that which Love and Reason should have done."[12] The only spirit that we can allow in the government of the church is a spirit consistent with that of our Lord.

4. We must aim to be the church and must never be content to remain a sect—but should offer an open hand to all God's people. Again I cite Baxter, who described his concern for "Catholic" Christianity in *The True Catholick.* Of that work, he said:

> It is for Catholicism against all Sects; to shew the Sin and Folly and Mischief of all Sects that would appropriate the Church to themselves, and trouble the world with the Question, Which of all these Parties is the Church? as if they knew not that the Catholick Church is *that whole* which containeth all the Parts, though some more pure and some less.[13]

Our aim is to be "catholic" in that sense, for only in that way can we fulfill our ecumenical mission.

Chapter 8
The Doctrine of the
Church (III)

The previous chapter ended with the principle of Catholicity in the church, and I want to suggest that that must be a further mark of our ecclesiology. We sometimes use the word catholic as if it were simply a synonym for "universal," so the "Holy Catholic and Apostolic Church" of the creeds becomes the "Holy Universal and Apostolic Church." I have already mentioned the universality of the church's message and outreach, and insofar as the word catholic means that, I have said enough.

But I suggest that it means more than that. It means not only the universality of its gospel and service, but also its comprehensiveness, its inclusiveness, its willingness to recognize as Christians and as potential members all those who confess the lordship of Jesus Christ. From the start it was a particular claim of Roman Catholicism and of those national churches that tried to hold under the one umbrella Christians of great variety. This is not simply to be dismissed as a political claim to be legally enforced, for there were many in the Established churches who recognized the attractiveness of the desire to be comprehensive. Sir Thomas Browne, a sixteenth-century Anglican layman, confessed that he was a member of "that reformed and new-cast Religion, wherein I mislike nothing but the name" and that was "of the same belief our Saviour taught, the Apostles disseminated, the Fathers authorized, and the Martyrs confirmed." He was not a Roman Catholic, but what was particularly attractive about his faith was his appreciation of Catholic devotion and his unwillingness to sneer at it or unchurch those who belonged to the Roman Catholic Church.

Thomas Browne admitted that he was naturally drawn "to that, which misguided zeale terms superstition" and clearly he was happy with the Anglican *via media,* but it is clear that his churchmanship included much more than a natural leaning toward liturgical forms. He admitted that his personal preferences for symbolism lay in that direction.

> At my devotion I love to use the civility of my knee, my hat, and hand, with all those outward and sensible motions, which may expresse, or promote my invisible devotion. I should violate my owne arme rather than a Church, nor willingly deface the memory of a Saint or Martyr. At the sight of a Crosse or Crucifix, I can dispence with my hat, but scarce with the thought and memory of my Saviour. . . . [And he admitted that during his travels in Europe] I could never hear the *Ave Maria* Bell without an elevation, or think it sufficient warrent, because they erred in one circumstance, for me to erre in all, that is in silence and dumb contempt.[1]

Obviously the quality of comprehension and inclusiveness in Sir Thomas Browne's churchmanship has nothing to do with indifference to religious differences or simple sentimentality toward Roman Catholics, but it was centered in Christian charity. And that is the fundamental reason why our churchmanship has to own the principle of comprehension and inclusiveness, for if we exclude even one sincere follower of our Lord from his table, we have come short of what the church should be.

However, it must not be imagined that we should all become Roman Catholics or Episcopalians because they profess to aim at catholicity. Indeed it should be clear from what we have just said about the Lord's Supper that we would have problems with "catholicity" as it is often practiced in those churches. Nevertheless, although we may differ about the theological basis of the catholicity held in those churches, and differ still more about the means used to achieve it at times in the past, their objective was right.

There are two areas in which this principle of catholicity becomes particularly important to our own redefinition of the doctrine of the Church.

THE ECUMENICAL GOAL

Two facts about the UCC have become apparent during its relatively brief history. First, it is clear that we were born with the ecumenical objective of trying to be a church that would invite others to participate with us in achieving the visible unity of Christians in the U.S.A. This was a laudable objective, but it is also clear that far from defining our position in society more precisely, the loss of the earlier ecclesiologies and the pursuit of a broader churchmanship have presented us with an identity crisis. As the ecumenical imperatives of the Vatican II era and early COCU gave place to other interests, the vision of Christian unity was lost in the fog of what appeared to be more pressing social issues. In many parts of the country we are none too sure any more who we are, and our name no longer seems to convey to people what it conveyed in 1957; I live in a part of the United States where the words Church of Christ in any church title suggest the opposite of the ecumenical goal and the liberal presuppositions that our members are expected to endorse.

In March 1979 there was a consultation on the problem of our polity and the identity problem in which we were caught. It was called by the Board for Homeland Ministries, and the keynote addresses were published in *New Conversations* (Fall 1979). If the ecumenical vision that inspired our original union remains a major objective of our church, then the principle of catholicity, inclusiveness, is vital to that goal, and it also has a curious effect on the problem of our present self-identity. Here is a small part of what I said on that occasion:

> We may have been looking at the question of a viable self-identity in the wrong sequence. In the days when our churches owned a distinctive polity—presbyterian or congregational—they based their distinctiveness on exclusive theologies, and we took pride in our exclusiveness and uniqueness. Today we are beginning to realize that pride of any kind is totally inappropriate to the Church of Jesus Christ. By the nature of our own ecumenical history and commitment, the search for a viable ecclesiology cannot be centered in a distinctively confessional doctrine of the Church. I have suggested that it will be found in a biblically grounded and (therefore) ecumenically directed theology, in a theology that ought to have equal claim on all followers of Jesus Christ without regard to denomination. We should no longer be looking for uniqueness and particularity, but for the forms of church life, worship and administration that most nearly point to the One who calls the Church into being.[2]

This implies catholicity because we want to belong to the "Great Church" in which all followers of our Lord will feel that they are welcome and belong: a church that maintains the ecumenical goal cannot be other than a community of faith that seeks catholicity in the fullest sense.

But the paradox is that this gives us a particularity that we do not seek, and we should work and pray for the time when it will disappear. The sooner it disappears, the more it will be to the credit of the whole Church.

In this time of continued separation and dividedness, however, the majority of churches are still tied to their traditional forms, and implicitly, to ecclesiologies that still take pride in their historical succession, their fidelity to the New Testament or Reformation patterns, or their possession of some distinctive gifts of the Spirit. The U.C.C. is a protest against this exclusivity in all its forms, and our testimony ought to be centered most visibly in our doctrine of the Church, in the kind of community we are. The United Church of Christ has little reason for a separate existence today, unless, *in the kind of church it tries to be,* it points all churches to the God of the biblical revelation who alone brings the One, Holy Catholic and Apostolic Church into being. Our ecclesiology should find its center in translating the meaning of our Lord's redemptive incarnation, life of service, sacrificial death and resurrection into terms of human community. And that begins where it began in the first century A.D. in the *acts* of those whom he calls to be his apostles.[3]

THE NEED FOR ECUMENICAL ORDERS

Because of the way in which Reformation conceptions of the church concentrated on the settled preaching and pastoral ministry, Protestant churches have had great difficulty in recognizing ministries that have not conformed to regular patterns of ministry to the Word and Sacrament. Those who have a clear sense of call but rather different gifts have found little recognition in our churches, and people who have a real vocation for Christian service, who might find a recognized form of service in one of the Catholic orders, discover that it is almost impossible to exercise any role commensurate with their spiritual gifts in the standard Protestant parish. The success of such experiments in ecumenical community as Taizé and Grandchamp in Europe illustrates the need, but there is little evidence that they would receive much support in the churches of American Protestantism: we cheer from a distance and return to the practical business of being what we have always been. But the issue is much broader than that of opening the door to celibate Protestant orders on the Taizé pattern; it is the problem of giving recognition to the gifts of the Spirit that do not fit our standard forms of ministry.

It is a dilemma that may be illustrated throughout the history of our churches since the Reformation. On the one hand the churches have received new life and vitality as committed and gifted individuals have seen a need and tried to address that need, which was not being addressed by the churches. On the other hand Protestant churches have not always known how to incorporate such prophetic movements into their life and witness, and sometimes this has forced such groups to justify their own existence by offering schismatic alternatives to the churches themselves: they have been forced into sectarianism.

Consider the extent to which Protestant churches have been in debt to nonecclesiastical movements that have arisen to meet specific tasks in the name of the gospel. This was particularly evident in the movements that arose out of the eighteenth-century and early nineteenth-century evangelical revivals, and a great deal of that Christian enterprise was directed to evangelism at a time when the regular churches had become so comfortable in society that not a few ministers regarded evangelism as close to heresy. Societies for evangelical work among the Jews, among city people and young people sprang up, and Bible societies for the production of Bibles. There were societies for the production of cheap Christian literature for those who had learned to read, and Sunday schools to give instruction to those who would not receive it in any other way. Home and foreign missions became the primary concern, and out of this missionary concern was born the social concern that tackled everything from the abolition of slavery and prison reform to caring for orphans and "fallen women." Foreign missions themselves extended their concern from the simple preaching of the gospel to medical missions, educational missions, and programs to improve the conditions of other peoples through the teaching of hygiene, irrigation methods, and simple engineering. The nineteenth century saw a remarkable expression of this kind of concern by individual Christians who banded together in ad hoc societies for the correction of specific abuses, for taking the gospel to neglected parts of society or the rest of the globe, or to testify to aspects of the gospel that were in danger of being ignored or misrepresented by the churches. Perhaps one of the best examples is that of the ecumenical movement itself, which was born out of the earlier missionary movement and out of the need to evangelize young people (the YMCA, the YWCA, and the WSCF).

Sometimes such movements won their way to acceptance by the churches, although it was usually against a great deal of initial opposition. It is clear that although Protestantism has constantly given birth to such movements and obviously benefited from their work, it has not been able to incorporate their gifts into the regular life and concern of the churches. Sometimes the movement that began quite happily by wishing to serve the whole Christian enterprise, in order to gain a place in our religiously pluralistic society, has been able to maintain itself only by becoming a new sect. The prime illustration of this may be in the story of the Wesleys and Methodism, but it was to be matched by that of William Booth and the founding of the Salvation Army (1878) and that of A.B. Simpson and the Christian and Missionary Alliance (1887). These provide us with examples of that kind of induced sectarianism. One wonders how Francis of Assisi would have fared in a Protestant society.

Sectarianism in all its forms has to be deplored for three reasons: (1) Because the sect tends to take its earlier *legitimate* concern and stress it to the point where it becomes a distortion. (2) Because the new sect, in order to claim its place as surrogate "church," has to become involved in things in which it lacks the wisdom and experience of the churches, and this deflects it from the mission in which it was making a genuine contribution. (3) In order to gain identity the sect tends to become exclusive toward the churches. The criticism (and often even its rejection) by the regular churches is deeply wounding, and this in reaction easily produces its own rejection of the churches.

The dilemma becomes a deep paradox when we reflect on the curious difficulty Protestant churches seem to have to reconcile the movements that they have constantly produced, and on which their own vitality has often depended, to the regular ministry of the church, and the comparative ease with which the Roman Catholic Church has been able to receive such work and ministry by creating special orders. Of course, the Roman Catholic Church has had some problems in this regard: it rejected the modernist movements in earlier days, and it has terminated the work of the worker priests, but at least it has had machinery for holding such movements within the system in a way that it does not force them to attempt a comprehensiveness and an exclusiveness that they are ill-fitted to claim.

I must admit that I do have a specific case in mind. For some years I have regularly taught church history to a group of young men and women who are dedicated to the task of working with high school students and leading them to the point of Christian commitment (Young Life). It is a task that our Christian education programs have signally failed to do. The movement is evangelical and tends to be conservative theologically, but not socially or politically. I have been permitted to teach my subject in precisely the same way that I would teach it in any "mainline" seminary, and both Protestants and Catholics have been included. Its leaders are certainly not Fundamentalists, although there may be extreme conservatism in its ranks, just as I suspect one might find the occasional member of the John Birch Society in the UCC.

What concerns me is that they are doing a job with young people that the churches, for the most part, are not doing, and the movement may be being pushed into sectarianism because the churches have no place for their kind of ministry. I am also concerned that those who are brought to a commitment to Jesus Christ by such means will be lost to the churches and will drift even further into exclusive sectarianism. We need to look at such movements with great care and compassion and, by holding out a hand of fellowship, explore the ways in which such special ministries might be recognized by the churches in a diaconate.

Chapter 9
The Place of Pragmatism

Because the Reformers and others were suspicious of human reason, the earlier ecclesiologies tried to exclude pragmatism from their consideration of the church's form. Luther and Calvin both have passages in which they castigate reason, and this rejection of our fallen faculties as reliable guides to divine truth was endorsed in our own day by Karl Barth's thunderous response to Emil Brunner, *"Nein!"*

This was a valid protest, for human history shows us that we are only too ready to turn human rationality into an ultimate authority that dismisses revealed truth and ultimately places human intelligence on the throne of the universe. When Lord Herbert of Cherbury began the movement that was to become deism by writing his *De Veritate* (1621)[1] and later his *De Religione Gentilium* (1663), his primary intention was not to undermine Christianity, but to discover a new basis for apologetic that could get rid of the religious prejudices of that time, and appeal to principles that were universal and equally true in any nation or culture. The end result of his work, however, was to undermine Christian faith because that faith is unalterably grounded in historical events that the church accepts as essential revelation. Revelation is essential in Christian faith, and there is no Christian faith without it. This is fundamental to our subject and something that no branches of the church need to hear more insistently than those that regard themselves as liberal. It is an essential aspect of the faith from those branches of the church that claim to be evangelical that deserves our attention: there is no gospel—no "good news"—if there is no revealed truth in Christ from God.

But where does revelation end and where do superstition, fusty tradition, cultural prejudices, and just plain bigotry take over? And how are we able to judge between the true and the false assertions of that which claims to be revealed orthodoxy? It is clear that in the seventeenth century, when Lord Cherbury was penning his protest, most churches regarded their own understanding of the church as essential Christian truth. That is why the arguments over the proper understanding of biblical texts between Congregationalists and Presbyterians were so bitter and so hotly contested. The Presbyterians had no compunction in claiming Acts 15 to prove their own authoritative system of church courts from local sessions to General Assemblies, while Congregationalists struggled to prove that, despite the thousands that entered the church after Pentecost, the church at Jerusalem could have comprised only a single church (i.e., congregation). The details of church government were extrapolated out of scripture as revealed truth, while others argued that because the divine revelation was to be seen in the Holy Spirit's continuing work in the historic church, all the details of Catholic practice must be maintained as necessary aspects of the true church of Jesus Christ.

Obviously we cannot justify that kind of detailed ecclesiology as God's revelation, for we have to admit that there are broad aspects of church government and practice that are grey areas, that have to be debated on purely practical grounds and accepted for their simple usefulness. But equally obviously we have to distinguish carefully between what is of divine institution in the ordering of the church and that which is held for practical (and therefore, temporary) reasons, lest we fall into a similar trap as churches in earlier times of creating a divinely sanctioned tradition out of elements that are occasional, temporary, and contingent.

What, then, are we to say about the use of pragmatism, reason, and common sense in the service of the church? I wish to offer a few basic principles under this head.

REASON IS THE GIFT FROM GOD

We do not need to apologize for the use of pragmatism in our churchmanship because God has given us our reason and intends that we should use it. This may sound elementary, but it is necessary to say it because sometimes theologians speak as if nothing in the church had been left for us to determine by ourselves. I can remember the shock I suffered when I realized that a place had to be made for the proper exercise of human reason in the work and organization of the church—a shock that was all the more traumatic because I had always stood with Barth against Brunner on the danger of allowing reason any authority in making our theological constructs.

But reason *is* God-given, and its own kind of authority cannot be denied. We cannot deny its operation even in areas that we would prefer to maintain as sacrosanct. Therefore, human reason cannot be rejected absolutely without denying an essential part of our humanness (and therefore our *responsibility*) that is the gift of God. As I have said elsewhere, "reason is a nontheological authority that enters into our understanding of the Holy Spirit's authority and of the means whereby the will of Christ has come down to us. It does so not as a foreign intrusion into our theological system, but because God wills us to be responsible and human." [2]

To push this further so that our understanding of it may be as clear as possible—reason is *necessarily* involved whenever we engage in exegeting the biblical evidence, or when we try to interpret the significance of the historical tradition, or when we try to work out the implications of our own spiritual experience. And when we work out the practical implications of the essentially theological enterprise of determining what our primary authorities have to say about the nature of the church, our reasoning becomes pragmatism.

However, this carries the inescapable implication that we can *never* regard our present understanding of the church in the fixed, infallible, and unalterable sense in which the doctrine of the Church was held in former times. If God has written our rationality into our situation so that we can make no theological conclusions without using the imperfect and fallen gift of human reason, it means that we can never make our present theological and ecclesiological conclusions absolute.

Because we are human, our reason is subject to all the same imperfections, prejudices, and plain human cussedness that fallen nature is heir to. It is certainly not infallible in its judgments about the divine revelation or impeccable in its attempts to express the will of God in institutional forms. Yet it stands apart from all our theological formulations and ecclesiological theories and "judges" them by God's own permission.

Therefore if human rationality occupies the position of an independent authority in relation to our theological constructions, God must be prepared for distinctively human imperfections to enter

91

into our understanding of the Church. Perhaps we are not intended to have infallible absolutes, any absolute authority through divine institution, sacred book, or inspired prophet to which we are expected to give the obedience due to God alone. That we have to recognize our own pragmatism at many points in the organization and operation of the institutional church *ought* to keep us from the danger of deifying one particular form of the Church. As A.R. Vidler observes, "No definitions made by the Church *in via* are in themselves final or irreformable, however faithfully they serve to mediate to mankind the final authority of God for practical purposes." Which seems to be another way of saying that a pilgrim people is called to walk by faith.[3]

We have to walk by faith, and we don't like that. We would rather walk by knowledge, preferably absolute and infallible knowledge. But the lessons shown by my own study of ecclesiology and the mistakes that have been made in the past force us to accept the challenge of being prepared to walk by faith with a new seriousness. And that apparently is the way God wants it.

THE PRAGMATISM OF THE GOSPEL

There is a pragmatism in the gospel that is endorsed by our Lord. "By their fruits ye shall know them [Matt. 7:20, KJV]" is the clear acceptance of the pragmatic principle in judging every kind of theological and ecclesiastical pretension, and it could not come from a better source. We do not need to apologize for using pragmatism in our churchmanship and laying down the rule of practicality. I suggest that this has not only to be recognized and admitted, but that it needs to be explicitly built into our theology of the church.[4]

Indeed, perhaps one of the reasons we have seen so much of the *wrong* kind of pragmatism in church history is that too often theologians have failed to recognize the theological place that practicality plays in our understanding of the church, and this may have led administrators and church leaders to introduce practical methods and considerations into church structure and programs in all sorts of illegitimate guises. There is no room for practical considerations in any view of the church that believes that Jesus laid down in detail the pattern of church government and practice. Repeatedly, in studying the Westminster Assembly, I found the divines arguing against any gaps in the biblical evidence regarding the church because, they reasoned, this would mean that the order Christ had left for the church was less complete than the government left for Israel in the Old Testament; and that could not be. Therefore, they were forced into the most extraordinary theological and exegetical gymnastics in order to fill those gaps. They forgot the gift at Pentecost.

Such convictions hardly did justice to their own Reformation position on the importance of faith, or to the biblical testimony that the gift of the Holy Spirit is at the very center of God's purpose for the church. If one examines (even on the basis of one's own literalism) the passages about the gift of the Comforter in the Fourth Gospel and the Epistles, one might be led to very different conclusions (i.e., that there was no need for church structure and practice to be laid down in detail precisely because the Holy Spirit had been given to the church to "guide it into all truth"). Although, as Christian disciples, our trust is wholly centered in Christ, our Lord himself trusts the influence of the Spirit in us. And that trust is fundamentally in the Holy Spirit's power to persuade faithful Christians to make the right practical decisions to further the work of the gospel.

The crucial words are "to further the work of the gospel." This is the difference between the right and the wrong kind of pragmatism in the church. It is not to be pragmatism for its own sake, or pragmatism for secondary reasons, but pragmatism *to further the work of the gospel.* And it is so easy to use practicality as an excuse for ends that are totally different, as history exemplifies only too well. It was undoubtedly the claim of most of the inquisitors in history, and at the center of the claim that "the end justifies the means." They assumed that the "end" was the success of the gospel, and therefore any practical way of achieving it was justified. But they did not see that in adopting those "means" the "end" changed and was no longer the victory of Jesus Christ, but the success of a "church" that identified Jesus Christ with bloodshed and torture.

Much the same can be said about Protestant history from the burning of Servetus in 1553, through the witch hunts and other forms of persecution in the early days, and the competitive diatribes of the later polemic, to the problems of our own century in which we so often choose the practical solution for the wrong reason. The claim to pragmatism often "has to be questioned, not primarily because it puts a premium on the practical, but because it so often loses touch with its spiritual source in Christ *and makes pragmatism an ultimate authority divorced from the gospel.*"[5]

The whole thrust of my argument is to assert without apology that practicality has its own proper place in our theology of the church, and that we do not ignore it without missing a vital element in what the New Testament has to say about the church, its structure and its mission. But the dangers of pursuing practicality for its own sake are so great that we have to be doubly sure that our motives are *Christian* when we invoke it. Before we make any claim that a particular "practical" solution will further the aims of the gospel, we should reread Gibson Winter's devastating critique of Protestantism's withdrawal from the inner city in the name of practicality in the 1950s[6]; as I expressed it earlier[7]:

> The Protestant churches had become concentrated in the suburbs, except for those churches—Ethnic, Black, Sectarian—which were tied to special groupings within the city. Mainline Protestantism was leaving the inner city spiritually destitute; and Winter showed us that as the inner city became more and more populated with those most heavily disadvantaged, a crisis in urban leadership was bound to descend upon the cities in which the churches of the exodus would be unrepresented and impotent. The cleavage in society was paralleled by a cleavage among the churches to the detriment of both: "The blue-collar and white-collar schism of the metropolis is thus crystallized in the schism between sectarian churches and the major denominations. This schism, as much a matter of style of life and culture as of economic interest, now cuts through the Negro community and complicates the division between Negro and White communities."[8] He made the prophecy in 1961—which all recent figures on the churches seem to support—that if the trend continued and a real ministry was denied the inner city, "within a score of years, Protestantism will be fatally weakened as a significant religious force in the United States."[9]

Our pragmatism must be uncompromisingly not only in the name of Jesus Christ, *but demonstrably and unambiguously in the Spirit of Jesus Christ*. If it is not, then however successful it appears to be in its practical results, it will ultimately be seen as blasphemy and will contribute to the huge credibility gap that has opened up for many between what the church claims to believe and what the church is in society. Spiritual pragmatism must constantly place itself under the judgment of the gospel, and that means placing itself under the Spirit of the One who was content to make himself of no reputation, but assumed the role of a servant and accepted that role in terms of the cross. There is no need to fear any pragmatism that holds that at its center.

OPENNESS TO CHANGE

It must follow that anything in church structure and government that is adopted to achieve the purposes of the gospel must hold itself open to the possibility of adaptation and change as the needs of the church's proclamation change. I do not believe that the forms of government that were appropriate and even necessary in the time of Ignatius of Antioch, or even in John Cotton's New England, are necessarily appropriate in twentieth-century America, or in the world megapolis that we may have to expect in the twenty-first century. Pragmatism has nothing to justify it if it fails to be practical! And this means that it must be constantly open to the need for change and adaptation as circumstances change.

It is difficult for church people to realize this because there seems to be an innate tendency for religious people to make a practical decision and then rationalize it into an ecclesiastical tradition that has to be passionately defended! Yet there are few things as ridiculous as to see a church, which has originally adopted certain practices for essentially pragmatic reasons, later developing an elaborate theological rationale to justify its practice, as if the action had been revealed to it by God! We insist that there is an important place for practicality in the biblical understanding of the church, but *because* of the essential constancy of God's own purpose toward creation, the church must constantly be alive to the need to translate that eternal and unchanging purpose into the terms demanded by our own changing historical situation. Certainly we must recognize the changeability of our practical decisions, and not invest them with a sanctity and permanence they do not have. If we are going to use pragmatism in the church's structures and methods, then there must be the clear understanding that the church at that point will be *semper reformanda*, always being reformed.

And perhaps there is no place in the church's life where members need to be kept more informed and instructed because it is one thing to see treasured customs and traditions being swept away in the name of a principle that is clearly more fundamentally part of our churchmanship, but it is an entirely different thing when we are asked to get rid of hallowed traditions and customs simply because someone at "headquarters" (or from even more nebulous regions) has said that we must. Nothing arouses local congregational anger more than the suggestion that they are being *told* to do anything. Our churches need careful and constant instruction in the basic biblical principles behind our ecclesiology, and by that I do not mean self-justifying memoranda sent down from "above," but regular instruction by ministers who are themselves theologically well informed. If you can show the biblical justification for an open attitude to change in our church structures and the biblical parameters of such change, then our people would be able to support any new policies that might be proposed; but until the time those things are defined and explained in a properly pastoral way, members have every right to resist changes they believe are being foisted on them at the mere whim of those who exercise the power.

PRAGMATISM, COMMON SENSE, AND THE DOCTRINE OF THE CHURCH

I have argued that since human reason is a God-given gift, we cannot ignore it in seeking authentic authority for Christian faith and action, and since pragmatism and common sense are the forms in which practical expression is given to rational decisions, they have a place in defining the authentic structure of the church for our own time. I submit that *jure divino* views of the church must always be subject to modification by pragmatic considerations.

But it is important that pragmatism itself and commonsense answers to practical problems are placed under the revealed authority we receive from the gospel itself. I have called this "evangelical pragmatism"[10] to distinguish it from the pragmatic attitude that is simply self-serving, an end in itself, or that promotes goals that are unworthy of the gospel. Yet the pragmatic principle in ecclesiology is of continuing importance because it encourages the flexibility in church structures that is necessary to meet the varying demands of mission.

A new spirit has recently appeared that points in this direction, and it has been shown in Third World approaches to the ecclesiological problem, particularly in Africa, where leaders are beginning to speak in terms of a contextual theology (i.e., requiring that the formulation of Christian doctrine reflect the needs and the idioms of the geographical and social context) in order to relate Christian truth more clearly to those contexts.

In the older churches, too, a trend has begun in this direction. Some have spoken of the period since the Reformation as the church's movement from an Aristotelian ecclesiology (to match the ancient Aristotelian or Ptolemaic cosmology) to a Copernican ecclesiology (and cosmology). Our twentieth-century problem is, however, that almost before we have begun to feel comfortable with the latter, we have had to readjust to the relativity of Einsteinian thinking and in order to meet it we have had to be ready for the total relativities (pluralism) of an "Einsteinian" ecclesiology.[11]

The intimate relationship of theology to cosmology seems to go back to the beginning of civilized thought (e.g., the Chaldeans, Egyptians, and then the Greeks).[12] Moreover, it is clear that the geocentric view of the universe was the most ancient, and therefore related to theological orthodoxy, by its association originally with the prestigious thought of Aristotle and then caught up in Ptolemy's encyclopedic *Almagest*. The views of Aristarchus, who had proposed a cosmic order much closer to the ideas we hold today, caused him to be accused of impiety, if not atheism. This identification of heterodox ideas of the cosmos with theological heresy was taken up into the thinking of the early Christian theologians. If the history of the church's relationships to science is taken into account, it seems clear that the place of rational thinking in our authority structure must be conceded. In relationship to the church and its institutions, this is pragmatism, and a place must be found for it in our ecclesiology.

The contextual concern seems to be the thrust of George Lindbeck's approach to doctrine in his book *The Nature of Doctrine*. Lindbeck's dissatisfaction with the traditional ways of defining doctrine is apparent from his opening paragraph.

This book is the product of a quarter century of growing dissatisfaction with the usual ways of thinking about those norms of communal belief and action which are generally spoken of as the doctrines or dogmas of churches. It has become apparent to me, during twenty-five years of involvement in ecumenical discussions and in teaching about the history and present status of doctrines, that those of us who are engaged in these activities lack adequate categories for conceptualizing the problems that arise. We are often unable, for example, to specify the criteria we implicitly employ when we say that some changes are faithful to a doctrinal tradition and others unfaithful, or some doctrinal differences are church-dividing and others not. Doctrines, in other words, do not behave the way they should, given our customary suppositions about the kinds of things they are. We clearly need new and better ways of understanding their nature and function.[13]

Later he describes three approaches to the definition of Christian doctrine: first, the earlier traditional (Catholic) approach to doctrine—the "cognitive-objective," followed by Reformation approaches—the "expressive-experiential." Both of these approaches may continue to have some validity for theologians, but Lindbeck feels that they cannot begin to meet the ecumenical needs of the present time. He therefore suggests that theology needs to adopt a third approach to truth—the "cultural-linguistic." This method has the advantage of maintaining the possibility of truth in all the options and refuses to categorize some as absolutely "right" and others as absolutely "wrong." Lindbeck observes that

Many modifications of common ways of thinking about religion follow from abandoning the notion that its source is in prior experience, but I shall mention only two. First, religious change or innovation must be understood, not as proceeding from new experiences, but as resulting from the interactions of a cultural-linguistic system with changing situations. Religious traditions are not transformed, abandoned, or replaced because of an upwelling of new or different ways of feeling about the self, world, or God, but because a religious interpretive scheme (embodied, as it always is, in religious practice and belief) develops anomalies in its application in new contexts. This produces, among other things, negative effects, negative experiences, even by the religion's own norms. Prophetic figures apprehend, often with dramatic vividness, how the inherited patterns of belief, practice, and ritual need to be (and can be) reminted. They discover the concepts that remove the anomalies. Religious experiences in the sense of feelings, sentiments, or emotions then result from the new conceptual patterns instead of being their source.[14]

If this is the direction in which global society is pushing us, then there are important implications for any future attempt to formulate the doctrine of the church and to translate that ecclesiology into practical structures.

1. Theologians will have to be much more careful about the order and form of the church that they are prepared to regard as absolutely required from the revealed source material; and perhaps they will have to be far less ready to regard such prerequisites as absolute for all time.

2. This demands flexibility in future church structures.

3. However, the approach also emphasizes our theological need to relate the givenness of the church's structure to its necessary flexibility (i.e., to relate what we believe about the revealed character of the church [cognitive doctrine from Bible or tradition] to the practical needs of the churches for their mission). This, in turn, underlines the need to take the classic doctrines and ecclesiology that we have received from our traditions with a fresh seriousness, so that our practical insights regarding the needs of the time are properly placed under revealed truth and do not try to supplant it.

Chapter 10
The Doctrine of the Church (IV): Two Ecclesiologies

J.C. Hoekendijk said that the church possesses nothing of itself, not even an ecclesiology,[1] and that is really a good summary of what I have been trying to say: everything that the church has *and is* points to God, and more specifically to "God in Christ": to Christology. As Forsyth put it, "that is the true Church, and the true form of the Church, that gives the best effect to the Gospel."[2] But whereas Jesus, by revealing himself to a specific time and place in history, was able to express Christology in a single personalized form, the same principle of redemptive incarnation for the church in history not only implies but demands freedom to adapt and become redemptively incarnate within the changing contexts.

But this thought contains its own set of problems, first, because the church is not Christ, and therefore cannot claim the perfection and infallibility that could be claimed by our Lord.[3] It points to Christ, but until the resurrection of all things it can never be completely identified with our Lord in those terms without deifying itself. Second, flexibility has to be balanced by order, for the church points not only to the continual willingness of God to seek and save this lost creation, but also to the changelessness of God's purpose. In his book *Do We Need the Church?*[4] Richard McBrien, one of the more radical Roman Catholic critics of Vatican II, used a perceptive analogy from the history of cosmology. He traced the transition of the church from what he called Ptolemaic ecclesiologies (in Trent and such writers as Bellarmine) to a Copernican ecclesiology, and he argued that as a result of Vatican II, the church lodged itself somewhere between the two. The problem was, he said, that the church of the future will actually need an Einsteinian ecclesiology.[5]

McBrien's imagery is significant. What he called "Ptolemaic" ecclesiology saw its theology as the all-important center around which everything else revolved and for which everything else subsisted. "Copernican" ecclesiology saw itself as existing among several equal planets revolving around the sun that warms all, although it might claim to be closer to the sun than all the rest. "Einsteinian" ecclesiology, however, would imply relativity in a cosmos without any recognizable center.

His imagery reminds us that changes in theology do reflect changes in the way people view their cosmos. To speak of an "Einsteinian" ecclesiology, with its implication of relativity, emphasizes that we live in a society where people recognize less and less any absolute values or any absolute authority behind those values. How do we determine the shape the church should take in the new circumstances? From the Third World countries we are getting the message that theology, and particularly ecclesiology, should be entirely contextual. We cannot ignore the contextual challenge to our understanding of the church. Furthermore, three decades of teaching church history in America have taught me that the American churches stand in a significant position between the older ecclesiologies of Europe and the contextual views of the church emphasized in Third World countries, since after the War of Independence all churches in America had to come to terms with their relationship to both their European background and the context of the young republic.

The issue raised by McBrien, however, forces us to ask the question whether a world view that has become completely relativized has any place for a doctrine of the Church. We must obviously be alive and sensitive to the way in which contemporary society views this world and its universe, but can we ever allow our theology to become *merely* the reflection of a contemporary world view? There is something uniquely theological to be said about humanity's place in creation and about human destiny. This inevitably involves what we have to say about the church and what we claim about its essential nature. But where do we get help? What is the relationship between the necessary flexibility the church needs to meet the varying social contexts in which it finds itself and its necessary dependence on an eternal and unchanging testimony to a purpose behind and beyond this cosmos in which relativity seems to rule? The first of these foci has to be sought in terms drawn from our contemporary world view; the second must always appeal to "revelation."[6]

At this point I return to two fascinating attempts to deal with this ecclesiological problem that arose from within or close to our own tradition during the past century. The Mercersburg movement tried to do it in the middle of the last century from within the German Reformed churches, and Peter Taylor Forsyth made the attempt from within British Congregationalism. Both of these efforts to recast our ecclesiology are remarkable for their agreements, and both deserve to be taken with seriousness in our attempt to do the same for our own time.

THE CHURCH IN MERCERSBURG THEOLOGY

The Mercersburg movement flourished during the years 1840 through 1870. I take as my terminus a quo the date of John Williamson Nevin's appointment as professor of theology at the Mercersburg Seminary and the terminus ad quem the date of Philip Schaff's transference to the faculty of Union Seminary, New York, although the movement had been in decline for some years. It is perhaps somewhat ironical that the Mercersburg theology is now best known for its liturgical reforms.[7] Ecclesiology always has liturgical implications, but liturgy of itself was not the primary concern of these men. As James Hastings Nichols has noted,

> what chiefly identified both Nevin and Schaff, in their own view and that of their contemporaries, was their interpretation of the Church. When Schaff first met Nevin he noted in his journal, "I feared I might not find any sympathy in him for my views of the Church; but I discover he occupies essentially the same ground that I do, and confirms me in my position."[8]

But before we delve into the actual ecclesiology, we should put the movement into its own historical context, for it was directly related to the circumstances of that time. We must recognize the traumatic effect on intelligent church leaders caused by the scientific and technological revolutions of the nineteenth century. We have become obsessed with the challenge of our own century, but the invention of steam power virtually changed the means of travel that had remained static since the invention of the wheel—horse by land and sail by sea—and the impact of Darwin's *Origin of Species* and the historical criticism of the scriptures inspired by Hegel's view of history questioned religious authorities that had remained unchallenged for practically 1,800 years. Even those who were prepared to accept the new knowledge felt a strong nostalgic tug, as we can see from some lines in Tennyson's *In Memoriam:*

> Let knowledge grow from more to more,
> But more of reverence in us dwell;
> That mind and soul, according well,
> May make *one music as before.*

In the last line (with my italics) one detects even in Tennyson a yearning for the reconciliation of religion and science enjoyed in earlier centuries.

For the church leaders of the nineteenth century, however, although the challenge of the scientific revolution may have constituted the most intractable problem, there were other threatening influences. The French Revolution produced an almost pathological fear among ecclesiastics in state churches that the church would become disestablished, and the *Communist Manifesto,* which inspired the revolutions of 1848, raised the specter of a total breakdown in Western society. Nostalgia for the earlier stability in church and state was one of the major factors that produced a reaction to the authority of church tradition, which we see in the Anglo-Catholic Tractarians; and in America the disestablishment and pluralism of post-revolutionary times were clearly seen by both Nevin and Schaff as a threat to the European churchly tradition of the Reformed churches. For both Nevin and Schaff the primary danger to the church seems to be focused in the individualism and sectarian tendencies of American revivalism.

Both men, however, became committed to the church through what were essentially pietist influences. Nichols says:

Schaff was a product of that Awakening which had begun on the Continent during the Napoleonic Wars. Swiss by birth, he owed his religious formation and his education to Swabian pietism. The pietist settlement at Kornthal prepared him for the university, and for two years at Tübingen (1837–39) he associated with the leaders of Württemburg pietism. Then at Halle, F.A.G. Tholuck (1799–1877), the leader of North German pietism, made him his secretary, and introduced the youngster, when he transferred to Berlin in 1840, to Baron von Kottwitz (1757–1843), the pietist patriarch of the Prussian capital.[9]

Schaff's more churchly concern came after the impact of this earlier commitment.

Much the same was true for Nevin, for he experienced "conversion" while he was a college student of seventeen, and although he was later to castigate the techniques of revival and condemn them as "Puritanism" (which he regarded as contradicting the essentially churchly character of "Reformed" faith), "he did not doubt that he had experienced a true awakening, which," as B.A. Gerrish has noted, "entered deeply into his subsequent history."[10] His reaction away from the methodology and individualism of evangelicalism was largely reinforced by his experiences at Princeton, and his growing conviction that the original ecclesial character of the Reformed position was being undermined by reliance on revivals and on such dubious techniques as "the anxious bench."

It is important, however, for us to recognize the earlier evangelical emphases on both Schaff and Nevin, lest we should misunderstand the significance of their later protest, or take their strictures against the "Puritanism" in American Protestantism altogether at face value. We should remind ourselves of the way the problem of authority affected post-Reformation Protestantism; as the doctrine of the Church became eroded, there was a tendency for Protestant theology to fly off into either an individualism of the head (rationalism) or an individualism of the heart (pietism), and as either of these emphases was pushed to excess, Protestant churches reacted by beginning to move in the opposite direction. This was certainly true of Puritanism, even as it had been true earlier of the continental churches.

The primary theological influence of the late eighteenth century had been in the direction of rationalism; deism was dominant throughout the period of the Enlightenment, and in America it produced transcendentalism and the unitarian split. Because of the new emphasis on the separation of church and state, and because their own doctrine of the Church had become somewhat eroded *by* their relationship to the New England states, the Puritan churches had turned in the pietist direction, as many of the Reformed churches of Europe had done in the late seventeenth century before them. Hence the emphasis on personal commitment and "conversion" that was to be found in mainline American Calvinists like Ashahel Nettleton and in the Presbyterian theologians at Princeton. They were reacting in the way we could expect them to react to the danger of rationalism.

This puts the Mercersburg theologians' own reaction to the prevailing mood in American Calvinism in its proper context. It *was* a reaction to the dominant trend to be found at that time in churches of

Puritan tradition. We can sympathize a great deal with their protests against the aberrations of later revivalism; but they were mistaken in thinking that the fault was endemic only to Puritanism. It is true that the Puritans may have been among the first in the Reformed churches to stress the importance of our *personal* commitment within the Covenant, but in earlier days that had always been balanced by the corporate discipline of the church. Indeed, as a corrective to the erroneous emphases of revival religion, it is interesting to note that Nevin applauds the catechetical method of Richard Baxter and cites the approval of Philip Dodderidge, two of the most representative Puritans of the seventeenth and eighteenth centuries.[11] The problem of the extreme individualism and its attendant emotionalism, against which the Mercersburg theologians rightly reacted, may arise in most forms of Christian churchmanship when the concept of the church has eroded

There is a striking parallel between their experience and that of leaders in the Anglo-Catholic Oxford (Tractarian) movement, such as J.H. Newman. Both Nevin and Schaff were immensely impressed by that movement, which—if one discounts the less attractive motivation of holding on to the status and privileges of the established Church of England—was largely a reaction against the individualism of the Evangelicals in England and a reassertion of the corporate discipline and faith of the historic church. It is worth noting that J.H. Newman's religious journey had begun in the conversion experience among Evangelicals. His brother, F.W. Newman, went through several contrasting "Phases of Faith," through the Plymouth Brethren, but ended as a Unitarian.

When we look at the earlier careers of Nevin and Schaff we see that they could hardly deny the place that personal commitment played in their spiritual journey. But their protest was simply that in the current state of religion in America, this individualism had become, for many, the whole gospel, and the holistic concept of the church had given place to a view in which everyone was supposed to have gone through precisely the same emotional experience.

It is wrong to take the Mercersburg theologians' strictures against Evangelicalism altogether at face value. They were all in its debt, but they were rightly protesting against the erosion of the doctrine of the Church and trying to recapture the *corporate* sense of the church's faith that was in danger of being lost among the discordant voices of individuals who were too busy shouting about their own personal faith. They represent a corrective. Personal faith *is* necessary, and this is something of which Evangelicals are right to remind us, but

Catholic movements of the church, such as the Tractarians and Mercersburg, are also right to insist that the corporate faith of the historic church always has priority over personal faith, that the faith for which the church throughout the ages has been prepared to suffer and die demands respect and (except in the rarest cases where one suspects a church may itself be in danger of apostasy) respectful allegiance.[12]

They were also right to insist that this sense of the historic church and its catholicity had been in the Reformed churches from their inception. Neither Calvin nor Zwingli (although they were less interested in the latter because of his eucharistic memorialism) thought of the Reformation as separating the churches from the life and history of the church that had gone before them. As the late Prof. Jacques Courvoisier of Geneva used to express it, the Reformation was intended to be only a marginal note in the history of the church.

It would be impossible in this study to attempt a complete survey of the Mercersburg theology in respect to its doctrine of the Church. However, there are four distinctive emphases about the church that are important for our approach to ecclesiology.

1. *The centrality of Christology and the incarnation.* The Mercersburg ecclesiology was essentially theological, in the fundamental sense I have interpreted "theology." Its absolute center was Christology and the doctrine of Incarnation, and if in that direction it drew all its theological significance from our Lord as the Incarnate Word, it also pointed in the other direction to the new humanity and the kingdom of God:

> The new creation is already at hand, not developed, indeed, to its last necessary results, but as an active force, all sufficient for its own ends, and really comprehended in the order of the world's history as it now stands. It is exhibited to us in the Church.
> The principle of this new creation is our Lord Jesus Christ. In him the Word became flesh, the divine nature was associated with the human as never before, and life and immortality were brought to light in our fallen world. The fact thus accomplished in his person was at the same time a fact for all time. It included in itself all the resources of life and salvation that were needed for the full redemption of humanity, onward to the grand millennial triumph in which it is destined to have its end. The Church, through all ages, is the depository of these resources. The life with which she is

filled, the powers that are lodged in her constitution, were all comprehended originally in the person of Jesus Christ, and are all still the revelation only of the grace and truth which came by him in the beginning. He is the alpha and the omega, the beginning and the end, of the Church, which is denominated on this account his body, the fullness of him that filleth all in all.[13]

This church, according to Nevin, is essentially the church of the historic creeds because it makes this confession in the flesh. The church is a *necessary* part of the gospel; indeed in one place he says that it is necessary to Christ because "Incarnation would be shorn of its meaning, if the fact were not carried to its proper world development, in the Church."[14]

2. *This church of the creed is Catholic.* What Nevin had to say about the essential catholicity of the church has particular relevance to us, both in respect to our commitment to Christian unity and in his insistence that the church not only bears testimony to the truth but is representative or exemplar of the truth.

First, in respect to our understanding of Christian unity, he insisted that "Catholicity" is an essential mark of the church.

Unity and universality belong not more essentially to the idea of humanity itself than they do to the conception of the Church; for this last is the form simply, in which the first is advanced to its ultimate significance, and thus made eternally complete. The Church must ever be one, even as Christ is one, and the whole world must be taken up organically, in the end, into her constitution. All this is involved in her very nature; and all this . . . is actually at hand also in the visible representation of her presence in the world. True, she is exhibited to us as in many respects a divided Church, and her catholicity is sorely marred, on every side, by forms of existence that contradict all such character. . . . But still she has the power by which in the end the entire world shall become new, outwardly as well as inwardly, in the harmonious unity of the Spirit.[15]

The first thing to note in this passage is the strong emphasis on the church as pointing to the kingdom of God and the fundamental unity of all humankind; and second, his emphasis on the *visible* unity of the church. This was quite unlike most Protestants of that time, who, when they spoke of unity at all, expounded it in terms of a purely spiritual unity. This was part of the evangelical legacy against which

Nevin was so scathing; today we would regard Christian unity as necessarily involving both.

But for all his Catholic preferences, Nevin never fell into the error of those forms of Catholicism that simply dismissed the "sects" as outside the Catholic Church, and therefore outside the realm of salvation. He insisted that even sectarian religion had to be regarded as organically belonging to the Catholic Church.

> We must believe that our sects, so far as they belong to the Church at all, belong to it organically, not as loose transports in its service simply, by which some of God's elect may happen to be conveyed to the heavenly Jerusalem, but as component portions of the one universal body of Jesus Christ in the world, representing collectively for the time, not separately, its life as a whole.[16]

In a lengthy footnote he recognized the tension in his position. "The sects then," he said, "are either not of the Church at all [the position taken by all other forms of Catholicism at that time], or they must be of it as so many outward totalities belonging to the body as a whole. How far the Church life may reach in this way, we cannot say."[17] It is clear from this that, much as he disapproved of "sects," Nevin did not fall into the trap of making his view of the church sectarian by limiting the Catholic Church to a single preferred form: Nevin had a concept of diversity in unity.

Second, he recognized that the *form* of the church was an indispensable and organic testimony to the Incarnation. The church, he said, "is not simply a witness to the truth as something lying beyond and outside of herself, but she comprehends and upholds the truth, in her own constitution, as being in the fullest sense the depository of the life of Christ himself."[18]

There are dangers, of course, in this position, particularly when it is made the basis of ecclesiastical triumphalism; and when that is linked to the power of the state, it may easily become the basis of a claim to impose dogma on a whole society, and even of a right to persecute those who differ. Within the American situation, however, with its constitutional insistence on the separation of church and state, there was less likelihood of that happening. The positive point that Nevin was making was that we cannot separate the form and the attitudes of the visible church from organic connection with its Lord.

At this point I should mention Nevin's distinction between the "ideal" church and the "actual" church. The Reformers had spoken about the "visible" and the "invisible" church, but Nevin preferred "ideal" and "actual," and he made a valuable contribution by showing how these are related to the "Holy, Catholic and Apostolic Church" of the creed.

> It is neither the Ideal Church, of course, nor the actual Church, separately taken, that forms the proper object of our faith, as expressed in the Creed, but the first as comprehended always in the second, and constituting with it the presence of a single life. In this view it is apprehended as a *real* Church, not a logical figment simply, nor yet the mere creature of human will, but a divine constitution actively present in the world, and steadily unfolding itself to its necessary end. As such, it is a *visible, catholic, historical,* and *life-bearing* Church, and is to be embraced in the way of faith accordingly.[19]

Nevin's distinction between the ideal church and the actual church may be of help to us, and particularly his insight that we are to think of the church wholly in terms of neither one nor the other, but in terms of their relationship.

But perhaps we have to rid ourselves of the triumphalism that all catholicizing movements of the nineteenth century tended to attach to the visible (actual) church, by reversing his way of presenting the issue. Our danger today is not that of spiritualizing the church to the point where the actual church becomes irrelevant, but of actualizing it and its visible unity to the point where the *ideal* has become irrelevant. I would rather suggest that we need to see the actual church in light of the ideal church; that is, we need to see the church as it is and the visible unity that we seek in the light of the church as it is spoken of in the gospel, as it is seen by God.

The triumphalism disappears if we recognize that the ultimate realization of the church *as it should be*, as the recipient of Christ's "glory," is never something that can be claimed for the church as it is here and now, but it is always a "becoming": the church of which we can say that it is "truly the mother of all her children," of which we can truly say that "they do not impart life to her, but she imparts life to them,"[20] is the actual church seen in terms of what it is to become, and the actual church as seen to be "ideal" only to God.

3. *The church is historical.* The church is historical in the sense that it has a continuous history since the time of Jesus and the apostles. That history is not to be denied, but there has often been the tendency in Protestantism to jump over the uncomfortable parts of church history in the hope of being able to restore the pristine

form of the church of the New Testament. We are debtors to the whole of that history. As Nevin observed:

> To suppose that it might make an entirely new start, under such a visible organic character, in the fourth century, or the sixteenth, or at any other time, springing directly from the Bible or heaven—its old life having failed altogether or run out unto universal apostacy—is most assuredly to belie its existence as a real Church entirely; as much so as to imagine any similar void or break in our common human life between its embryo formation in the womb and the full maturity of manhood would be plainly to convert the whole process into a mere Gnostic phantom. We may allow the Church to have become in certain periods very corrupt and false to her proper character, but let us beware of annihilating in thought her outward, visible, organic perpetuity. That were a heresy of a very serious and grievous order.[21]

This aspect of the Mercersburg ecclesiology received especially detailed treatment in the studies of the historian Philip Schaff, and if his material is read with care, we can see how several aspects of the Mercersburg movement—particularly its criticisms of the prevailing patterns of American Protestantism at that time—are to be understood not as absolute positions, but as correctives to the popular mood.

In the introductory section of his *Geschichte der christlichen Kirche; Erster Band: Die apostolische Kirche* (1851) (translated as *History of the Apostolic Church with a General Introduction to Church History*, by E.D. Yeomans, 1853), Schaff discerned three periods in the history of the church: (1) a period in which there had been a union between the objective and the subjective in the church, when "the authority of the general [community] and the freedom of the individual appear tolerably balanced"[22]; (2) a period when objectivity had dominated, and which had produced "the age of *Christian legalism*, of *Church authority*," when personal freedom had been, to a large degree, "lost in slavish subjection to fixed, traditional rules and forms";[23] and (3) the period that began with the Reformation, in which subjectivity and individuality had taken precedence.

The quality that constituted the strength of Protestantism also was its weakness, and it was this which was to be seen in the Anglo-Saxon forms that prevailed in North America.

> In North America, under the banner of full religious freedom, it has reached its height; but in its essence, it belongs to Protestant

Christianity as a whole. All our Protestantism is sadly wanting in unity, at least in outward, visible unity, which is as necessary a fruit of inward unity as works of faith. The sects, indeed, do not commonly reject the Bible. On the contrary, they stiffly adhere to it, in their own way. But they rely on it in opposition to all history, and in the conceit that they alone are in possession of its true sense. Thus their appealing to the Bible, after all, practically amounts in the end to rationalism; since by the Bible they always mean *their own sense* of it, and thus in fact follow merely their private judgment.[24]

Here Schaff saw quite clearly the basic problem in all forms of biblical restorationism, for instead of the Bible becoming the final authority as the Word of God, the end of the process gave final authority not to the *Word* in the scriptures, but to our human understanding.

A careful reading of his introduction to church history shows that far from wishing to destroy completely the subjective, individual apprehension of faith, he wished simply to get rid of the perversions that arose when this was made the supreme criterion of religion. He wanted to apply a proper corrective in the corporate faith of the whole church and argued that this was the only proper context in which our own personal faith could grow.

4. *The life of the church is dynamic.* It is dynamic because it is divine, and it is divine because it is centered in the Incarnation. "Christianity," Nevin said, "strictly speaking is not a system of doctrines, nor a code of ethical rules, nor a record of events long past or passing at the present time, but it is a perpetual fact, that starts in the Incarnation of the Son of God."[25] Therefore the living powers that the church possesses "are not indeed the product properly of the Church outwardly considered; they spring perpetually from Christ himself, as the vitality of the body descends into it from the head. They are present, too, always and only in the presence of the Holy Ghost."[26]

At first sight this seems to place the function of the Holy Spirit in a subordinate role, until we reflect that the Fourth Gospel points out that the Spirit's primary function is to reveal the things of Christ and make them known to the church (John 14:26; 15:27; 16:13f.). Nevin saw everything in the church in terms of Incarnation; it gave him his high view of the ministry, and it was at the center of his view of the sacraments. In words that were almost a prophecy of what would be said by P.T. Forsyth in very different circumstances and half a century later, he declared: "The sacraments in particular have a living power in themselves. They are not signs and shadows only, like the symbols of Freemasonry or Odd-Fellowship but a divine life is actually comprehended in them for the high supernatural ends they are designed to serve."[27] Further in his essay on "Wilberforce on the Incarnation" (1850) he said: "The idea of the Church, as standing between Christ and single Christians, implies of necessity visible organization, common worship, a regular public ministry and ritual, and to crown all, especially, grace-bearing sacraments."[28] The liturgical aspect of Mercersburg was thus set within the context of the church, and that points to Jesus, and supremely to his Incarnation. As Nevin said in the Wilberforce essay:

> The true order of the Christian faith is given in the Creed. All rests on the mystery of the Incarnation. *That* is itself Christianity, the true idea of the gospel, the new world of grace and truth, in which the discord of sin, the vanity of nature, the reign of death, are brought for ever to an end. Here is the order of life which was not in the world before, the Word made flesh, God and man brought into living union in the person of Jesus Christ, as the nucleus and fountain of salvation for the race. He is the mediator, because God and man are thus in a real way joined together and made one in this person.[29]

As James Hastings Nichols observed, Nevin "laid his emphasis on the Person rather than the work of Christ, the Incarnation rather than the atoning death, and this ran counter to the prevailing evangelical theology."[30]

When we have made due allowance for the need to counter the enthusiastic overemphasis of "the prevailing evangelical theology" on the atonement, I would still have to part company with Nevin at this point. It is, I submit, dangerous to separate the Incarnation and the Atonement, or so to emphasize the one that it virtually incorporates the other. It was precisely this that has led some forms of "Catholicism" to argue from the Incarnation to the church in a way that claimed Christ's own perfection and infallibility for the church itself, and to argue from this also to a view of the sacraments that almost invested the elements themselves with divinity through the words of consecration. True, the Atonement would not have happened unless the Incarnation had taken place; but given the situation of the world and of our human race, would the birth of Jesus Christ have been incarnation if it had not issued in atonement?

I prefer to hold the two doctrines together and speak of the *redemptive* incarnation. The Incarnation of Jesus Christ is to be understood as the New Testament writers came to understand it—as the revelation of God's redemptive purpose—and the church is only a continuation of that Incarnation as it continues that redemptive purpose. To suggest anything else is to invest it with a divine claim that our Lord never made for himself. In the same way with the sacraments; they are the continuation of the *magnalia dei*, the mighty *deeds* of God[31]: it is more than presence, it is presence *for the purpose of redemption*, as our own UCC Statement of Faith makes clear. The Mercersburg theologians were right to center in the Incarnation, and they were justified in protesting against the death-centered theology of the contemporary evangelicalism, but in emphasizing Incarnation to the point where Christ's presence alone *becomes* sufficient atonement, they may have stepped across a boundary beyond which there was the idol of a deified church.

THE DOCTRINE OF THE CHURCH IN PETER TAYLOR FORSYTH

Forsyth belongs to a generation after Mercersburg, for he was born about the time that movement was beginning (1843) and he died about the time Karl Barth was publishing his great commentary on Romans (1921). The main part of his career was therefore spent at a time when the churches were beginning to feel more comfortable with the results of biblical criticism—indeed, when they were beginning to feel so comfortable that they were in danger of exchanging the assurance that twentieth-century science could bring in the kingdom here and now for the promises of the biblical revelation. For all his debt to the critical scholarship of Germany, and for all his willingness to be counted in the liberal camp, Forsyth spent the last thirty years of his life protesting against the antitheological, non-biblical forms of religion that he saw appearing within Protestantism, and therefore he speaks to us with a particular pertinence regarding the dangers of our century. He wrote these words in 1916, in the middle of World War I:

The nemesis of an anti-theological religion is that it has no resources in a crisis except pale Quietism or ruddy patriotism. It follows the saint or the drum. It retires among the mystics, or it goes out with a flushed nationalism. But its scale of business cannot handle large orders. It has not the resources for a foreign trade. It gravitates to the retail business. It has more instinct for missions, for instance, than power to maintain them or manage them. . . . To drop the metaphor, the attractive piety of incipient culture, with its atmosphere of young bustle, good form, gentle faith, genial love, kindly conference, and popular publications, is without the great note of New Testament realism and imagination; and it is therefore at an utter loss when the world is shocked and forced upon the question of a theodicy. What can it do in the swellings of Jordan?[32]

For those to whom Peter Taylor Forsyth is perhaps little more than a name, I should say something of his career. He was born into a home of respectable poverty in Aberdeen, Scotland, where his parents belonged to the Congregational Church. It should be noted that Scottish Congregationalism had an entirely separate origin and existence from English Congregationalism. It was an indigenous restorationist movement that had arisen through the Evangelical revivals at the end of the eighteenth and beginning of the nineteenth centuries, and it was associated with the preaching of two laymen, the Haldane brothers: Robert (1764–1842) and James Alexander (1768–1851). The Haldanes also influenced the future work of the young Scots-Irishman Thomas Campbell, and this influence would be carried to the American frontier.

In line with the Scottish tradition, poverty was no bar to an education for anyone who had ability, and young Forsyth won his way to Aberdeen University, gaining distinction in Classics and becoming an assistant lecturer in Latin. Then, on the advice of Robertson Smith, he went to Göttingen for a semester, to make acquaintance with German theology, and he studied under Albrecht Ritschl. He returned to Britain and applied to New College, London, to train for the Congregational ministry, but ill health appears to have interfered with his training. He eventually held pastorates near Bradford, in Yorkshire, and at Hackney, in North London, but in neither the Yorkshire Union (i.e., Association) nor the London Union was his ministry fully recognized by the Calvinist churches of nineteenth-century England, probably because they suspected his orthodoxy.

But as in the case of Barth a generation later, it was in the course of caring for souls in the parish that Forsyth's theological conversion took place. He was brought face to face with the reality of God's grace. He did not give up his commitment to honest critical study of the scriptures but recognized a prior commitment to God's grace in Jesus Christ. He gave a moving account of how this happened in his Lyman Beecher Lectures, offered to the Yale seminary students in 1907, and published the next year as *Positive Preaching and the Modern Mind*[33]:

What has often passed as the new theology is no more, sometimes, than a theology of fatigue, or a theology of the press, or a theology of views, or a theology of revolt. Or it is an accommodation theology, a theology accommodated only to the actual interests of the cultured hour. . . . The tongue is new enough, but it is not certain that it speaks the old thing, or develops its position from a profounder acquaintance with the holiness of the love of God within the Cross. It analyzes the Bible, but it does not reconstruct from the Bible, but from what is known as the Christian principle, which is mainly human nature re-edited and bowdlerised.

I am sure no new theology can really be theology, whatever its novelty, unless it express and develop the old faith which made those theologies that are now old the mightiest things of the age when they were new.[34]

In 1894 Forsyth became minister of Emmanuel Congregational Church, Cambridge, and soon after he arrived there his wife died; but although he was "a tired and sick man," he began to receive some recognition.[35] Aberdeen honored him with a doctor of divinity degree the next year, and he was invited to preach a sermon for the Assembly of the Congregational Union of England and Wales. This was an extremely powerful sermon on "The Holy Father," and has been described as "a glorious exposition of God's grace."[36] The holiness of God was perhaps the dominant theme in Forsyth's theology and was at the heart of his desire to ethicize theology. He began to be listened to. At that time he saw, perhaps more deeply than any of his contemporaries, the basic problems that faced the churches, particularly the centrality of the need for a spiritual authority to take the place of the church's earlier reliance on either the authority of the church or the literal words of the scriptures. This issue he addressed in "The Evangelical Conception of Authority," delivered to the International Congregational Council at Boston in 1899.[37] Two years later he was invited to become principal of Hackney College, a small, impoverished Congregational seminary in North London.

This was Forsyth's first and only theological appointment, and it came when he was already fifty-three years of age. He held it until his

115

death in 1921. He was at once caught up in the struggle between the old conservatives and the new liberals that was a major preoccupation of British churches at that time. The significance of his position was that he refused to be absolutely identified with either party. He accepted the honest results of scientific criticism, but he rejected the vapid theological reconstructions of the "New Theology." He entered into a long and sometimes somewhat acrimonious debate with one of his friends, R.J. Campbell, who was regarded as the founder of the New Theology. When Campbell began to publicize his views in the national press, Forsyth remarked that the New Theology reminded him of a bad photograph; "it was underdeveloped and overexposed."

Like the theology of the Mercersburg theologians, the theology of P.T. Forsyth should have a particular significance for us because it tries to be loyal to the deepest insights of the older Reformed orthodoxies while accepting the best insights from the new scientific method, and like the earlier work it carried this basic characteristic of Reformed theology so that it presents an *integrated* theology: all the parts belong to one another, and that means that it deserves much more thorough treatment than can be offered in a work of this kind. Forsyth's work on the Church should be seen in relation to his concern about the issue of authority, his Christology,[38] his understanding of God's grace, the Incarnation, and the work of Christ, and his attempt to relate this to Christian social action.[39]

However, he did deal specifically with the nature of the church in *Lectures on the Church and the Sacraments*,[40] which was surely one of the most significant ecumenical statements to appear out of his church in this century. Perhaps the best way to introduce the modern reader, unacquainted with Forsyth, to his distinctive emphases in this matter is to quote the opening words of his own preface to that work.

My position is neither current Anglican nor popular Protestant. I write from the Free Church camp, but not from any recognized Free Church position—having regard, so far as I can, to the merits of the case, to early history, and to the experience of religion. The ruling tendency is an effort to moralize this and other parts of theology by interpreting instead of abolishing.

The view here taken is neither memorial and Zwinglian nor is it High Catholic. It is sacramental but not sacramentarian, effective but not sacrificial. The elements are not emblems but symbols, and symbols not as mere channels, but in the active sense that something is done as well as conveyed. . . . The audience is Free Church, but the treatment means to be Great Church.[41]

The term Great Church occurs often in Forsyth's writings, and it is his term for the One Holy Catholic and Apostolic Church of which the creeds speak. There is a particularly striking passage in which the "Great Church" appears in *Positive Preaching and the Modern Mind*, when he shows the relationship between the work of a pastor in the local congregation and the faith of the Holy Catholic Church.

The business of each pastor in charge of a flock is to translate to his small flock this message and content of the great Church, that he may integrate the small Church into the great, and that he and it together may swell the transmission of the Word in the world. That is the true Catholicism, the universalizing of the universal Word. That is the principle which makes a Church out of a sect or conventicle, and puts a preacher in the true apostolic succession. The true succession is the true inheritance of the eternal Word, and not the true concatenation of its agents. The great apostolate is one, not in heredity of a historic line but in solidarity of a historic Gospel, not in a continuous stream but in an organic Word.[42]

Of course, one must recognize that Forsyth was protesting against the forms of Catholicism that interpreted catholicity wholly in terms of the legality of a particular form of ordination, but one should also see that he left little room for the kind of Protestant sectarianism that ignores the faith of the rest of the church in history.

We should remember that at that time there was a great deal in both British and American society that caused Congregationalists and those of similar churchmanship to preen themselves as being most in line with the democratic tendencies of the time. Forsyth warned them against such an alliance with any cultural context.

Democracy, after all, is but another of the ocracies which have come to the top in the history of mankind; and it is not the last. Despotism, monarchy, aristocracy, plutocracy, and so forth—they have all had their hour. And the Church at the last has had to resist every one of them, though it has, more or less, succumbed to every one. . . . Does the society of Christ depend for its life and right on the goodwill of any society of men in the world? Sooner or later a great struggle will come between the Church and the natural democracy; and then those Churches which, being super-natural in principle, have yet in practice become dependent on that democracy, will find themselves stripped of their support, torn asunder, and distressed beyond measure.[43]

Much more fundamentally, he reminded the churches that

> the first condition of religion is authority. It is an authority before it is a liberty. The fundamental difference between a Church and a democracy lies thus in the principle that no numbers can create real authority such as the Church confesses, whereas democracy as such will listen to no authority but what its numbers and majorities do create.[44]

Because of the catholic view he had of the Great Church, and because he refused to become caught up in the democratic preferences of his society, Forsyth insisted that the preacher was to reflect the faith of the Great Church and the views of neither his own congregation nor even of his particular denomination. The preacher is "the mandatory of the great Church, which any congregation or sect but represents here and now. And what he has to do is to nourish that single and accidental community with the essence of the Church universal."[45]

From the same perspective he castigated the tendency to atomism—he called it "granular autonomy"—of local congregations that during the nineteenth century had become for many Congregationalists the cherished center of their ecclesiology, in the name of a far greater autonomy, the autonomy of God as Sovereign. He declared:

> Local autonomy is only sound and valid as it serves the supreme autonomy of the Great Church amid the powers of this world. . . . Autonomy can easily run down into anarchy if it is not a constant reflection of the *absolute* holiness and *free* grace of God in His Kingdom. It must be created from that. It must live in the autonomy, the self-determination, of the One God and His Grace.[46]

Forsyth maintained that no form of the church is given to us for all time. And yet this does not mean that the way in which the church is organized or the forms it adopts in worship and administration are irrelevant; in the following passage he was particularly scathing toward the free church tendency to discard ancient forms too easily or to encourage casual forms of worship.

No form is sacrosanct. But also to discard form is suicidal. If an imperial Church is mischievous, sporadic churches are futile. For a Church to live anyhow is to die. To abandon all noble forms of worship and to potter at it in dressing-gown and slippers, as it were, and to do this as a principle, in the name of independence, is to subside into hugger-mugger at the end in spite of any mysticism. Free prayer by all means, if you can keep it up. But few can pray in public, and they need help. No public body can afford to live in its shirt-sleeves, and pick up its meals, to disregard its social ritual and live casually. Certainly no Church can go on doing so with its creative spiritual wealth. Here the form can never be independent of the content. To abjure entirely Church authority and the solemn tradition of the worshipping dead in worship or doctrine is to slip down into a heap of sand. No authority, no Church. Loose procedure means slack belief. And slack belief means loss of public influence for the Kingdom of God. . . . The Reformers found a Church dead one way; but they replaced it by a Church which, on the Lutheran side at least, was in another century dead in the other way. And it has never there regained, as a Church, spiritual life; while Calvin held the glorious West in fee.[47]

I feel that Forsyth here wrote off German Lutheranism too easily in his desire perhaps to commend the work of Calvin: after all, Calvinist scholasticism fell into similar errors to those of Lutheranism. But we remember that 1916 was a time when British church leaders were none too sympathetic to the state church of Kaiser Wilhelm.

At the same time his major insight is surely sound; forms of worship that ignore the liturgical traditions of the past are ultimately sterile: theological renewal will inevitably produce liturgical renewal. This was to be amply demonstrated within the Congregational churches of England later in this century.[48]

There is one point at which Forsyth's theology seems to cut across the theology of the Mercersburg theologians. He was extremely chary of regarding the church as a continuation of the Incarnation because he saw that in certain forms of Catholicism this had magnified the church to the point where it had virtually become deified. It is tempting to argue from the *perfection* of our Lord himself to the perfection and infallibility of the church as his Body, but Forsyth saw this as a grave danger. He wrestled with the idea of the church as the continuation of the Incarnation in one of his most important and closely reasoned passages in *The Church and the Sacraments*.

There is a way of magnifying the dignity of the Church which, in seeming to glorify Christ in it, yet destroys the true relation with its Lord. Is the Church in history the *prolongation* of the Incarnation? It is an attractive imagination. It is the Catholic form of the engaging fallacy of liberalism that Christ is but the eternal God-in-man, supremely revealed and carried to a luminous head in Him, but forming always the spirit of Humanity and looking out in every great soul. But if the Church is this, can we also call it the Body of Christ? For when Christ became incarnate, His soul took a material body . . . whereas the Church in which Christ dwells is not a material body, but an organism of spirits. In the Incarnation Christ passed into a flesh distinct from Himself Who took the resolve so to pass. It was distinct from Himself because at the proper time he separated from it, and it became a corpse. But in the Church He passes into living souls capable of a moral reciprocity of which the body of His Incarnation was incapable. His earthly body could not love and trust Him as His Church does. . . . The Church He created cannot be a continuation of Him the increate. And that externalising went so far as that He took the body in which human nature itself is externalised. But the Church is not Christ's body in that material sense. Nor is human nature in its psychological sense the body of Christ; for it has to be reborn. It is regenerated human nature in which Christ dwells. But that cannot be a prolongation of His Incarnation, wherein there was no regeneration. His great spiritual work was not the result of a regeneration, but the source of it, as the Church cannot be. His externalisation in the Church took the form of souls outside Himself yet in Him newborn, and, though united with Him, not merged, as corporal substance might be. The interpenetrating personalities yet subsist as such. He is still outwardly present in Church and Sacraments, but present as He is not in nature, whether human or material. He is present as He can only be present in moral beings who have in grace left nature behind.[49]

He thought that the idea of the church as a prolongation of the Incarnation

lends itself too readily to a view of the Church as the mere evolution of Christ, which squeezes the notion of a new creation outside. No. To express this second form of His outward presence, the Church, we need some other word than the prolongation of the Incarnation, and one that does more justice to the cruciality of the Cross and the reality of the New Creation. The doctrine of Redemption is signally absent from the creeds, yet the Church has a more direct connection with Redemption than with Incarnation. Only by experience of Redemption has it a religious knowledge of what Incarnation means.[50]

There are three things to be pointed out about this passage.

1. Forsyth was rightly concerned to avoid the triumphalism that invades our thinking about the church when we *claim* that the church as we know it is a continuation of the incarnate perfection of our Lord. After writing once about the church as the Body of Christ I received a letter from Nathaniel Micklem, formerly principal of Mansfield College, Oxford, warning me that it is correct to use it as a metaphor as it was used by Paul, but it becomes dangerous when we interpret that metaphor as metaphysical truth. Forsyth was wrestling with this, and therefore he insisted that in relation to the church the Incarnation has to be seen in relation to the Atonement. If the church is to be considered as a continuation in any sense of that which became incarnate in Jesus Christ, it is a continuation of *redemptive* incarnation.[51]

2. In his legitimate fear of deifying the church, Forsyth may have tended to downplay the features of the church that are essential vehicles of our Lord's incarnate presence among us. The church is more than "an organism of spirits." If the church to be the church has to be "reborn," this rebirth is enshrined within human bodies of flesh and blood.

In the sight of God, the church *is* a continuation of Christ's redemptive Incarnation—a translation into corporate terms of that which our Lord's redemptive life and actions made incarnate. But there is a whole universe of difference between the way in which God's grace views the church and what the church may claim for itself. Indeed, to make claims for the church as if the church-that-we-know is as perfect as the church-known-to-God is to manifest a spirit that contradicts the gospel and is to invalidate the very claims that we have made.

3. The emphasis on redemptive incarnation leads directly to what Forsyth had to say about the sacraments.

Perhaps we should start with what Forsyth had to say about the ministry: "We can never sever that great impressive idea of a real Sacrament from the idea of the ministry. Without that conveying power in the end it is nothing."[52] "The Church," he said, "will be what its ministry makes it."[53] The ministry "has not to be directly effective on the world so much as to make a Church that is. It has not to reform the world, but to create a Church for the world's reformation."[54] The ministry is "God's gift to His Church."[55]

He castigated what he called the "laicising of the ministry"[56] and thought that the downgrading of the ministry was all of a piece with "the Zwinglianism which makes the Supper a mere memorial, or like the historicism which reduces the Bible from a sacrament to a document":

> No wonder the ministry is lightly treated if it is viewed as a mere convenience, like a chairman, as the proposer of the adoption of the divine report. And in quarters it is so viewed. Some preaching is like proposing the health of the gospel. Some prayer is like moving a vote of thanks to the Almighty, with a request for favours to come. Some ministry is but a facility. There are those who look on the minister simply as one of the members of the Church—the talking or the presiding member. They think anything else spoils him as a brother. They believe a Church could go on without a minister, only not so well, with less decency and order.
>
> That is all wrong. The minister is much more than a leading brother as the Church itself is more than a fraternity. He is neither the mouthpiece of the Church, nor its chairman, nor its secretary. He is not the servant, not the employee, of the Church. He is an apostle to it, the mouthpiece of Christ's gospel to it, the servant of the Word and not of the Church; he serves the Church only for that sake. The ministry is a prophetic and sacramental office. . . .[57]
>
> The ministry is sacramental to the Church as the Church itself is sacramental to the world. For the Church is sacramental as a living element and vehicle of Christ's redeeming grace.[58]

With this as preface it will come as no surprise to find that Forsyth had a "high church" view of the sacraments. He said, "Let us at least get rid of the idea which has impoverished worship beyond measure, that the act is mainly commemorative. No Church can live on that. How can we have a mere memorial of one who is still alive, still our life, still present with us and acting in us? Symbol is a better word than memorial," but then he went on to declare:

> A Sacrament is as much more than a symbol as a symbol is more than a memorial. It is quite inadequate to speak of the Sacrament as an object-lesson—as if its purpose were to convey new truth instead of the living Redeemer. It is not an hour of instruction but of communion. It is an act, not a lesson; and it is not a spectacle nor a ceremony. It does something. It is an *opus operatum*. More, it is an act of the Church more than of the individual. Further still, it is an act created by the eternal Act of Christ which made and makes the Church. At the last it is the act of Christ present in the Church, which does not so much live as Christ lives in it. It is

Christ's act offering Himself to men rather than the act of the Church offering Christ to God. Now, as at the first, it is Christ giving over to men the sacrifice He was making once for all to God. So that we may say this. The elements are symbolic only in the modern sense of the word symbol—only as signs. They convey nothing. They point to the significate but do not include it. But the action (of the Church and chiefly of Christ in the Church) is symbolic in the greater and older sense in which the symbol contains and conveys the significate, and is a really sacramental thing. Christ offers anew to us, as He did at the Supper, the finished offering which on the Cross He gave to God once for all. . . .[59]

One error of the Mass is that the priest offers God. But no man can offer God; God offers Himself. He makes the sacrifice. He did in Christ, and He always does. In prayer we go to God, in Sacrament He comes to us. The Sacrament is not an occasion of offering even ourselves to God, nor chiefly of our presenting Christ's offering; but it is an occasion of God in Christ offering, giving Himself anew to us in His Church.[60]

Word and Sacrament belong together because "the great sacrament of Christianity is the sacrament of the living and preached Word of Reconciliation, whether by speech, rite, or work. The elements may be anything; the Word is everything, the active Word of God's Act, Christ's personal Act met by His Church's."[61]

The sacraments are at the center of the church's worship,[62] and it is clear that he believed strongly in the Real Presence, but he shows his distinctively Protestant emphasis by accenting the *action* in the sacraments. Just as redemptive action reveals the Christ within the church, so the real presence of Christ is to be seen not so much in the elements themselves, but what is done in them. "The great matter is to recognize the real Presence in holy and saving action,"[63] and this is the theme to which he repeatedly returns in this book: "This brings us to the kind of redemption which centres in a historic act. . . . The holy sacrament is the sacrament of the holiest act and not simply of a most sacred essence or even presence."[64] At that point perhaps he went beyond Nevin, but if he did, this simply underlines how important it is to make our *theology* of the Church clear; for whether we start from Incarnation or Atonement, Nevin and Forsyth would have agreed that there is no other place to begin our ecclesiology than from the affirmation that "God was in Christ reconciling the world to himself."

Epilogue

I am not sure whether we should call these final comments Epilogue. It might be more appropriate to regard them as the preface to a work in which the whole of our church should be engaged.

It should be clear from the foregoing that the history of the UCC prevents it from having any single fixed pattern of ecclesiology as part of its essential dogma. I would also further submit that we are not committed to any single and unalterable pattern of church government. However, this does not mean that we are left without theological guidelines in helping us to determine the shape of the church in the future.

1. Although there is no single ecclesiastical form arising out of our own history that commits us to a particular polity, we do have, first, a historical priority to follow a form of church government that gives to each and every member his or her proper respect and due; and second, an ecumenical priority to adopt a form of the church that will enable us to press toward the ultimate unity of all Christians.

2. This ecumenical priority also means that we should treat all forms of the church arising from the traditional authorities with seriousness.

3. Obviously there is, within our history, that which demands that we should give careful attention to the patterns of church government to be found in the scriptures. As I have said elsewhere, "we are to be biblically based but not biblically bound." We are concerned less with the exact pattern (or rather, patterns) of the church in the New Testament than with the spirit that permeated the New Testament churches.

4. Similarly we respect the tradition of the whole church and accept its guidance as the corporate testimony to the truth of Christian doctrine. Although we do not feel bound necessarily to follow the shape that the church has developed in history, we recognize that

this constitutes a valuable testimony to the way in which Christians have tried to put themselves corporately under the Spirit of God.

5. But we would also insist that we cannot put boundaries on the work of the Holy Spirit: "The spirit bloweth where it listeth." Therefore there must be freedom in church structures to adapt ecclesiastical forms to meet the needs of the institutional church in each succeeding age.

6. I also insist that there is a place for what I earlier called "evangelical pragmatism." Human rationality is not an absolute authority, but it is a God-given gift, and we would hold that it may be applied to the needs of ministry and evangelism in any age, as long as it is made to serve the ends of the gospel and does not become an end in itself.

7. The most important principle that arises from UCC history is that ecclesiology should be governed by Christology and theology. The shape of ministry is obviously derived from the ministry of Jesus. Christology also points us to a ministry that is essentially both prophetic and priestly. Similarly the church must move toward becoming a communal expression of the character of the God revealed to us in the scriptures.

Perhaps the most important insight for our day arising out of our reflections on the nature of the church in history is the suggestion that the church exists to express the Christian life in corporate terms: "The Church was founded to be Christ-in-community, and this is the one thing which our Lord left his Church to contribute to the gospel: it was to be a reconciled community exercising a ministry of reconciliation."[1]

The foregoing helps to explain certain characteristics of UCC practice that may have remained a mystery to many of our members.

1. Because we take the New Testament witness with great seriousness, we cannot ignore the gift of the Holy Spirit to the church. And because we are concerned primarily with the Spirit in scripture rather than with finding proof texts, we cannot be bound to a static form of the church that remains unchanged in history. But the unwillingness to establish a fixed form of the church should be seen not as laxity or as unwillingness to take a stand, but should be understood as a desire to have theological integrity: we worship the living God. The dynamic view that we have of the God in scripture can be expressed only in a dynamic view of the church.

2. We cannot separate what we believe from how we act because,

in the Bible, God reveals the divine nature in terms of things *done*. This is one of the most important emphases in our own Statement of Faith.

3. So also we have to see that ecclesiastical forms reflect God's own inclusiveness toward those who have been dispossessed or depressed. Our ecclesiology will therefore have to be wide enough to recognize all the world's need. The same theological principle prevents us from making any false distinctions between men and women, even when such distinctions appear to be supported by a literal appeal to particular scriptural verses.

Ecclesiology is not an end in itself; it points to the kingdom of God and to the manifestation of that kingdom in human society. Our emphasis on the corporateness of the church is because it is through its corporateness that the church can most directly help society to become what God always intended that it should become.

This does not offer us a clear-cut pattern of ecclesiology, but as we bring these insights together, we can see why our ecclesiology continues to have distinctive features. Our aim in ecclesiology should be to ensure that in form as well as in profession our church should reflect the nature of the God revealed to us in the scriptures. The form of the church should reflect particularly the spirit in which God acts in history rather than try to reproduce within the twentieth century strict allegiance to scriptural patterns for the church.

Appendix
The Autonomy of the Local
Church: Historical Perspective

Nothing has raised more heat and given more problems to the emerging ecclesiology of the UCC than the autonomy of the local church. Indeed, it is doubtful whether, without the concession of this principle, the UCC would ever have got off the ground. In the original *Constitution and Bylaws* the principle was clearly set down in Article IV, Section 21. In the most recent edition (1984) it appears in Article IV, Section 15:

The autonomy of the local church is inherent and modifiable only by its own action. Nothing in this Constitution and the Bylaws of the United Church of Christ shall destroy or limit the right of each local church to continue to operate in the way customary to it; nor shall be construed as giving to the General Synod, or to any Conference or Association now, or at any future time, the power to abridge or impair the autonomy of any local church in the management of its own affairs, which affairs include, but are not limited to, the right to retain or adopt its own methods of organization, worship and education; to retain or secure its own charter and name; to adopt its own constitution and bylaws; to formulate its own covenants and confessions of faith; to admit members in its own way and to provide for their discipline or dismissal; to call or dismiss its pastor or pastors by such procedure as it shall determine; to acquire, own, manage and dispose of property and funds; to control its own benevolences; and to withdraw by its own decision from the United Church of Christ at anytime without forfeiture of ownership or control of any real or personal property owned by it.

Let me start with a double confession: much of this appendix appeared first as a paper given to the former Theological Commission of the UCC. Second, if I seem to concentrate unfairly on Congregational history, it is not due to confessional chauvinism, but to the fact that the autonomy of the local church "derives from the Congregational line of our inheritance."[1] This is where the issue was generated.

First, however, let us look at the Evangelical and Reformed tradition in order to make this clear. The E & R Church was presbyterial in structure, and to that extent the balance of authority (and even of power) was on the side of the judicatories. According to *The Constitution and the By-Laws of the Evangelical and Reformed Church*,[2] a congregation consisted of baptized and confirmed members who "live sober, righteous and godly lives and labor faithfully to bring others to Christ" (p. 7, Sections 8–9); these members also were to accept "the standards of faith and doctrine prescribed in the constitution of the Church" and were to be "organized and governed in accordance with the provisions of the constitution and by-laws" (p. 6, Section 7). We can therefore fairly confidently appeal to that document in defining the relationship between the local congregation and the judicatories.

In the E & R Church, congregations constituted the synods, and these in turn, through elected delegates, formed the General Synod (p. 10, Section 22), and "a judicatory shall have only such authority and powers as are committed to it by the body which creates it" (p. 10, Section 23). But although, theoretically, it would seem that authority was passed *from* the local up to the regional and national organs, in fact authority was exercised in the opposite direction. Matters of church discipline were handled initially by the Spiritual Council of the parish in the case of lay members, but by the synod for ministers. It is explicitly stated that "the Synod shall have legislative, administrative and judicial functions" (p. 11, Section 28), and that "it shall have jurisdiction over its ministers and congregations" (ibid., Section 29). The structure of authority continued through the General Synod, the supreme legislative body of the E & R Church, which regulated its judicial procedure (p. 12, Section 33). It is clear that the General Synod and its Judicial Committee was the highest court of the Church (pp. 48–54, "Discipline and Judicial Procedure"), and that therefore the local congregation was "under" the spiritual jurisdiction of the synod and the General Synod.

The same was true with regard to the administration and ownership of its material assets. Although a congregation was able to adopt its own constitution and bylaws (as long as they were in general accord with those prescribed by General Synod), and although it held its property through local trustees, it was clearly stated that when any congregation dissolved, the synod would have control of its members, property, and records (pp. 16, 22, Sections 15, 47). Therefore it appears that from the E & R tradition, the local congregation did not enjoy absolute autonomy and was subject to the Church's judicatories.

Conversely, the independence and autonomy of the local church (congregation) has always been near the central nerve of Congregational churchmanship, although the Theological Commission was perfectly right to point out that it was not until the nineteenth century that the principle was expressed as the "autonomy" of the local congregation.[3] The historical roots are, however, much more complex than most Congregationalists (or ex-Congregationalists) are ready to admit.

Unlike the E & R tradition, which was a direct inheritor of the continental Reformation, Congregationalism has its raison d'être in ecclesiology, and it arrived on these shores *because* of its ecclesiological differences with the established Church of England. Its members took a "high church" position in that they stood for the *jure divino* form of the church set down in the New Testament.[4] This basic congregational view of the church is illustrated in the four assertions with which Henry Jacob prefaced his *Reasons* in 1604.[5] Assertion No. 4 was, of course, the clincher: "The ordinary forme of Church government set forth unto us in the New Testament, ought necessarily to be kept still by us." It should be pointed out that Jacob was not a Separatist, but is regarded by modern historians as a principal actor in establishing the non-Separatist Congregationalism that later settled itself in Massachusetts Bay Colony.[6]

Congregationalism made its point of departure from this restorationist doctrine of the Church, which it claimed was instituted by Christ and was binding on the church for all time. The issue of local church autonomy has to be seen within this context, more particularly because comparatively few modern Congregationalists subscribe to the biblical literalism on which it was based, and therefore maintain the principle of autonomy on very different grounds from those established by their forebears in the faith.

The historical position is complicated somewhat by the separate history of Congregationalism in England and America, but more particularly by the fact that congregational polity was professed by both Separatist and non-Separatist congregations.[7] Although twentieth-century Congregationalism in both England and America represented a fusion of Separatist and non-Separatist influences, some tried to disparage one or the other branch of the tradition for political reasons. The debate usually centered in the autonomy of the local congregation and its relationship to the denominational representative synods, associations, assemblies, or councils,[8] and the UCC inherits the suspicion that this policy sometimes caused. If it intends to deal honestly with the issue of local autonomy, it will have to take both streams of Congregationalism seriously.

In fact, the Separatist position professed by Robert Browne was not so very different from the position that was taken by people like Henry Jacob. Look at Browne's definition of the church, quoted earlier.[9] Browne decidedly did *not* represent the atomistic independency that is often represented as the Separatist position. He recognized a fellowship of churches and the necessity for synods: "There be Synodes or the meetings of sundrie churches: which are when the weaker churches seeke helpe of the stronger, for deciding or redressing of matters: or else the stronger looke to them for redresse."[10] He defined a Synod as *"a Ioyning or partaking of the authoritie of manie Churches* mette togither in peace, for redresse and deciding of matters which cannot wel be otherwise taken vp,"[11] and if this stopped short of presbyterial power, it is not very different from the position taken by the exponents of the New England Way. True, Congregational Puritans, while emphasizing the final authority of the local covenanted congregation under God, were more specific in the authority they gave to synods, granting them the right to withdraw fellowship from an errant congregation but stopping short of the presbyterial right of excommunication. Thomas Hooker, in 1645, expressed the position for them all.

A Church Congregationall is the first subject of the keys.

Each Congregation compleatly constituted of all Officers, hath sufficient power in her self, to exercize the power of the keyes, and all Church discipline, in all the censures thereof.

Ordination is not before election. . . .

The consent of the people gives a causall vertue to the compleating of the sentence of excommunication.

Whilst the Church remains a true Church of Christ, it doth not lose this power, nor can it lawfully be taken away.

Consociations of Churches should be used, as occasion doth require.

Such consociations and Synods have allowance to counsell and admonish other Churches, as the case may require.

And if they grow obstinate in errour or sinful miscarriages, they should renounce the right hand of fellowship with them.

But they have no power to excommunicate.

Nor do their constitutions binde formaliter & juridice.[12]

The principle of the local congregation's spiritual autonomy was firmly established in the representative writers in both England and America, and in every official declaration of polity from the Cambridge Platform (1648, New England) and the Savoy Declaration (1659, Old England) to the Constitution of the UCC (Article IV, Section 21).

"All Congregationalists," says Increase Mather, "deny that Synods have any such ('judicial') power." "What is the power of a Council," says John Norton, "To declare the truth, not to exercise authority." Hooker "denies a Synod that hath a juridical power," but admits "one of counsel." "The sentence of a Council," says Richard Mather, "is of itself only advice, not of itself authority nor necessity." "It belongeth unto Synods . . . not to exercise . . . any act of Church authority or jurisdiction," says Cambridge Platform. "When a Church wants light," said Davenport, "she should send for counsel, but preserve the power entirely in her own hands." Cotton Mather's *Ratio* (himself rather bending towards Presbyterianism) says, "They pretend unto no judicial power, nor any significancy, but what is merely instructive and suasory." "When they (Councils) have done all, the Churches are still free," says Samuel Mather, in 1738, "to accept or refuse their advice." President Stiles says, "Churches universally hold a negative on the result of Council; the decision of a Council is of no force till received and ratified by the inviting Church, nor does it render that Church obnoxious to community, if she recedes from advice of Council." "It is an acknowledged principle," says Upham's *Ratio*, "in respect to Councils, that they possess only advisory powers." "Congregationalists, however, agree in asserting that Councils have neither legislative nor executive authority over the Churches," says Punchard. Emmons is still more explicit.[13]

I do not think that Robert Browne would have found much in this with which to disagree.

For all this unanimous testimony to the spiritual independence of the covenanted congregation, it is, however, clear that local autonomy does not abrogate other aspects of the church. Despite the fact that the Presbyterians dubbed them "Independents" and were able to make the nickname stick, our forebears on both sides of the Atlantic were unanimous in their detestation of the term.[14] They had other insights into the gospel, and although the independence of the local congregation became primary for historical and political reasons, it was held together with these other insights.

THE PRINCIPLE OF MINISTERIAL AUTHORITY

Perry Miller, who was rightly ironic about the direct line that former historians drew between the New England Way and post-Jeffersonian American democracy, pointed out that Congregational New England was governed as a close-knit oligarchy.[15] For all the right of the congregation to elect its officers and to admit or dismiss members, control was firmly in the hands of the church officers, once elected. Ministers were the experts, the reverend lawyers who defined, expounded, and administered the divine law.

Robert Browne may have originally "intended matters of rule to be determined by the whole body of the saints,"[16] but his successors, whether Separatist (John Robinson) or Puritan (Henry Jacob), held that once officers were elected, the people ought simply to submit and be obedient. For example, Jacob suggested that although final authority was in the hands of the congregation, the members should avoid initiating matters themselves and he expected them "freely to consent to their Guides preparing & directing every matter."[17] Miller quotes an intriguing letter from Thomas Weld in which Weld described how he and his colleagues avoided trouble by bringing "as few matters as possible, into the Assembly, rather labouring to take all things up in private, and then make as short work in publique (when they must needs come there) as may be."[18] No "open process" in the Puritan churches.

Clearly there was a form of congregational "prelacy" that went a long way to abrogate the autonomy of the local congregation, although I doubt whether it could (openly) be admitted or commended by many Congregationalists since that time.

There was a further New Testament insight that prevented this tendency from developing, and sent New England Congregationalism in a different direction. This was the conviction that the authority exercised in the church must take its character from the

Christian gospel; it must be "ministerial" rather than "magisterial," persuasive rather than coercive, redemptive rather than punitive. So John Cotton, in his Introduction to John Norton's *Responsio*, declared: "Church government is not an authority but a ministry. Let the kings of the earth fight for their authorities, for the lands and boundaries of their jurisdiction, but among ministers of the Lord Jesus the greatest is as the least and as he that serveth."[19] Cotton and his colleagues may not have always exemplified this standard, but he was enunciating a principle that was consistently held in their ecclesiology, and one of great ecumenical significance.[20] Furthermore, in its denial of coercive *power*, it was a principle that prevented ministerial authority and expertise from overriding the guidance of the Holy Spirit in the congregation or destroying its corporate authority.

THE PRINCIPLE OF INTERCHURCH FELLOWSHIP

This principle was exemplified in the Congregational synod. Robert Browne gave a good description of the synod and its nature—churches meeting together in peace "for redresse and deciding of matters which can not wel be otherwise taken vp," and as the opportunity for weaker and stronger churches to support one another mutually in the faith.

But again the quality or character of authority exercised by a synod was persuasive and ministerial. In the event of a congregation becoming hopelessly heretical or schismatic, all means of persuasion were to be used, short of force, to convince the members to recognize the error of their ways, but if they continued to be intransigent, the other members of the synod simply withdrew the community that had already been broken.[21] The synod was therefore seen not as an encroachment on a local congregation's responsibility to organize its own life under Christ, but as an extension of the Christian family. Basically the synod was the opportunity for responsible, self-governing,[22] equal congregations, which owned the same covenant of grace, to take counsel and encouragement together—an expression of what the Eastern Orthodox call *sobornost*—but this autonomy has to be understood within a wider context and within a mutual ministry of concern.

133

THE PRINCIPLE OF CONSENSUS

In his description of Elizabethan Separatism, Perry Miller put his finger on a crucially important principle for understanding local autonomy in Congregational history. He pointed out that since in every congregation the rules of Christ and Christ's Word "were held to be explicit and all-sufficient, and were to be administered by God's chosen people, there would be complete unanimity. Ecclesiastical overseers were unnecessary."[23]

This was also a basic presupposition of the Puritans, and although the authority assumed by ministers suggests that the expectation became somewhat tarnished in New England, it was clearly at the center of their conviction that ecclesiastical uniformity could be established and maintained. If the Bible presented a clear pattern of churchmanship, there was obviously no excuse for deviation from the rule, and where there were obscurities, they expected the Holy Spirit to lead the churches into a consensus beyond individual differences of interpretation.

This simplistic approach sustained unity in the New England Way until the Great Awakening, but the biblical literalism on which it was based is no longer viable. Then what about their expectation that the Holy Spirit would lead God's people into unanimity beyond their differences? Is there any common basis of interpretation on which a consensus could be sought at the present time, or does the principle of consensus have no practical value for us? We recognize that an enforced uniformity of belief and practice is neither desirable nor Christian, and if "consensus" means "compromise," there is little to commend it at any time: but would it be possible for our churches voluntarily to self-limit their autonomy in order to seek truth that goes beyond the polarities of majority and minority opinion? These are questions that the Puritan tradition puts clearly to us.

We are met by an entirely different climate in the nineteenth century. The inroads of science, and the problems caused by an America that was rapidly expanding geographically and economically, would eventually break the monolithic structure of Calvinistic orthodoxy, but the situation also offered exciting possibilities for the redefinition of Christian faith. Ecclesiology was under somewhat similar pressures: polity became political in a new sense, for in the idealism of the new American republic, the church was viewed less as the prophecy of a kingdom beyond time than as the earnest of a society that was in process of appearing here and now. The question of local autonomy, no less than the other "democratic" aspects of Congregational ecclesiology, seemed to find new and relevant justification in post-Jeffersonian democracy and in the material prospects of individual enterprise. It was no longer centered in the Crown Rights of the Redeemer in his Church, but in the emerging ideals of the new national society.[24] I suggest that the strong statements defending "the autonomy of the local congregation" leading up into the Burial Hill Declaration of 1865 and the foundation of the National Council of Congregational Churches in the United States in 1871 should be read in the light of that changing context.

At the same time, the evangelical challenge offered by the frontier, by the massive nineteenth-century immigration, and by industrialization and urbanization helped to liberate the earlier ecclesiology from its exclusivism and to develop its latent ecumenism. The Savoy Declaration of England in 1659 had made a tentative and somewhat amusing move in this direction when it provided that "Churches gathered and walking according to the mind of Christ, judging other Churches (though less pure) to be true Churches, may receive unto occasional communion with them such Members of those Churches as are credibly testified to be godly and to live without offence."[25] The recognition of a wider ecclesiastical pluralism—implicit in an ecclesiology centered in free and equal congregations—received explicit expression when Noah Porter's provision was accepted into the Burial Hill Declaration:

We rejoice that, through the influence of our free system of apostolic order, we can hold fellowship with all who acknowledge Christ; and act efficiently in the work of restoring unity to the divided Church, and bringing back harmony and peace among all "who love our Lord Jesus in sincerity."

Thus recognizing the unity of the Church of Christ in all the world, and knowing that we are but one branch of Christ's people, while adhering to our own peculiar faith and order, we extend to all believers the hand of Christian fellowship, upon the basis of those great fundamental truths in which all Christians should agree.[26]

This represented a radical shift from the *ex jure divino* ecclesiology of original congregationalism that was never frankly faced, nor has serious attention been given to the fact that when the freedom of the gathered church under Christ became "the autonomy of the local congregation," it exchanged a view of the church based on divine right for one based on a political or even a secular understanding of religious pluralism.

Perhaps for these reasons, and in view of the fears engendered by proposals to organize as a national denomination, the "autonomy of the local congregation" was carefully safeguarded in all the moves leading up to the foundation of the National Council of Congregational Churches in the United States.[27] Within the past hundred years no feature of Congregational Church life has been guarded more jealously than this.

As the pressures toward intradenominational cooperation increased, it was probably inevitable. Americans noted with great interest that the principle had also been safeguarded through the formation of the Congregational Union of England and Wales (CUEW) in 1831, and the success of that venture was of considerable influence in the establishment of the National Council in 1871. It has been pointed out that the constitution of the CUEW contained a clause that in substance "has been written into all constitutions, British or American, adopted since":

I. That it is highly desirable and important to establish a Union of the Congregational Churches and Ministers throughout England and Wales, founded on a full recognition of their own distinctive principle, namely, the scriptural right of every separate church to maintain perfect independence in the government and administration of its own particular affairs; *and, therefore, that the Union shall not in any case assume legislative authority, or become a court of appeal.*[28]

The intention of the italicized clause is clear—to assure nineteenth-century Congregationalists that there was no intention of establishing a national representative body that would then, or at any stage in the future, threaten the autonomy of the local churches in the denomination.

What the nineteenth-century leaders in England and America did not foresee was that they had set in motion an ecumenical concept of the church that might call this principle of local autonomy into question for the sake of the very catholicity they were beginning to recognize, and in the name of the same gospel that the principle of autonomy was intended to express. The United Church of Christ has inherited that legacy of ecclesiastical paradox.

Notes

Introduction

1. Robert McAfee Brown, *The Significance of the Church* (Philadelphia: Westminster Press, 1956), p. 17.

Chapter 1   The Doctrine of the Church

1. Quoted from the *Oxford English Dictionary*, ad loc.

2. *A Booke Which Sheweth the life and manners of all true Christians* (Middleburgh, 1582) #35; Albert Peel and Leland Carlson, eds., *The Writings of Robert Harrison and Robert Browne* (London: George Allen & Unwin, 1953), p. 253.

3. Claude Welch, *The Reality of the Church* (New York: Charles Scribner's Sons, 1958). The quotation is from the publisher's comment.

4. Robert McAfee Brown, *The Significance of the Church* (Philadelphia: Westminster Press, 1956).

5. Emil Brunner, *The Misunderstanding of the Church* (London: Lutterworth Press, 1952).

6. Daniel Jenkins, *The Strangeness of the Church* (Garden City, NY: Doubleday, 1955).

7. J.A.T. Robinson, *Honest to God* (Philadelphia: Westminster Press, 1963).

8. Luther J. Binkley, *The Mercersburg Theology* (Manheim, PA: The Sentinel Press, 1953), p. 109.

9. Robert S. Paul, *Ministry* (Grand Rapids, MI: Wm. B. Eerdmans, 1965).

10. Robert S. Paul, *The Church in Search of Its Self* (Grand Rapids, MI: Wm. B. Eerdmans, 1972).

11. Ernst Troeltsch, *Die Soziallehren der Christlichen Kirchen und Gruppen* [1911]. It appeared in English as *The Social Teaching of the Christian Churches*, trans. Olive Wyon (New York: Macmillan, 1931).

12. Cf. my two books cited in the notes above and also the following

articles: "The Unity of the Church—Quo Vadis?" *Midstream*, vol. 14, no. 1; "Ecumenical Vision in the 1970s," *Midstream*, vol. 16, no. 2; "Where We Begin: Freedom and Responsibility in the U.C.C.," *New Conversations*, vol. 2, no. 4 (Fall 1979). I hope to be able to bring all these thoughts together in a book on the twentieth-century quest for authority.

Chapter 2   Our Inherited Ecclesiologies: The Evangelical Traditions

1. Theodore E. Schmauk, in Introduction to *Works of Martin Luther* (Philadelphia: Muhlenberg Press, 1943). Hereafter cited *PE*. I:330.
2. Luther, *PE*, I:249.
3. Robert S. Paul, *The Church in Search of Its Self* (Grand Rapids, MI: Wm. B. Eerdmans, 1972), p. 132.
4. *PE*, I:361. Weimar Edition (hereafter cited *WA*), VI:301.
5. *Luther's Works*, ed. Jaroslav Pelikan and Helmut T. Lehmann. (Philadelphia: Fortress Press, 1955-), XL:34f. Hereafter cited *LW*. *WA*, XII:189f.
6. *LW*, XL:40; *WA*, XII:193.
7. Ibid.
8. Introduction to "Church and Ministry," *LW*, XL:x.
9. Cf. Paul, *The Church in Search of Its Self*, op. cit., p. 134, n. 35; p. 136, n. 43.

Chapter 3   Our Inherited Ecclesiologies: The Reformed Traditions

1. Cf. *The Assembly of the Lord: Politics and Religion in the Westminster Assembly and the "Grand Debate"* (Edinburgh: T.&T. Clark, 1985).
2. Article 1; cf. J.P. Kenyon, *The Stuart Constitution* (London: Cambridge University Press, 1966), p. 264.
3. The *Reasons*, A 1, verso.
4. Ibid., p. 25, E 1, recto.
5. *Jus Divinum Regiminis Ecclesiastici*, pp. 53f. Italics mine.
6. Gisbert Voet, in Hans von Schubert, *Outlines of Church History* (English translation, London, 1907), p. 288.
7. Congregationalists, for example, could point validly to Calvin's insistence on the place of the people in the election of church officers and in discipline (IV, iii, 15; xi, 5), while Presbyterians would naturally approve his emphasis on the authority of the ordained ministry and his identification of the New Testament bishop and presbyter as one and the same office.
8. *Institutes*, IV, i, 1. (References are to book, chapter, and section.) Quotations are from the translation of Ford Lewis Battles in vols. XX and XXI of the "Library of Christian Classics," ed. John T. McNeil (Philadelphia: Westminster Press, 1960).

9. Ibid., IV, i, 1.
10. Ibid., IV, i, 2.
11. Ibid., IV, i, 3.
12. Ibid., IV, i, 4.
13. Ibid., IV, i, 5 and 6.
14. Ibid., IV, i, 7.
15. Ibid., IV, i, 8.
16. Ibid., IV, i, 9.
17. Ibid., IV, i, 10–16.
18. Ibid., IV, i, 17–29.
19. Ibid., IV, iii, 1–3.
20. Ibid., IV, iii, 4.
21. Ibid., IV, iii, 4.
22. It has been pointed out that Calvin called Luther "a distinguished apostle of Christ by whose ministry the light of the gospel has shone." (F.L. Battles, *Institutes*, II: 1057, n. 4: Calvin, *Defensio adversus Pighium* [C.R. VI, 250]. Calvin was also aware of the evangelists active in America.
23. *Institutes*, IV, iii, 5.
24. Ibid., IV, iii, 5 and 6.
25. Ibid., IV, iii, 7.
26. Ibid., IV, iii, 9.
27. Ibid., IV, iii, 10.
28. Ibid., IV, iii, 11.
29. Ibid., IV, iii, 13.
30. Ibid., IV, iii, 15.
31. Ibid., IV, x, 27–32.
32. Ibid., IV, x, 27.
33. Ibid., IV, x, 29.
34. Ibid., IV, x, 30.
35. Ibid., IV, x, 32.
36. Ibid., IV, xi, 1.
37. Ibid., IV, xi, 5.
38. Ibid.
39. *Letters*, cf. the references in *Institutes*, II: 1218, n. 11.
40. *Institutes*, IV, xi, 6. In the same passage he suggests the distinction between preaching and ruling elders.
41. Ibid., IV, xii, 4. Also in a later section, using Cyprian as his authority, he writes: "Although the bishop with his clergy possessed a power of reconciliation, it required at the same time the consent of the people, as Cyprian elsewhere shows." Ibid., IV, xii, 6, citing the same passage from the *Letters* mentioned above.
42. *Institutes*, IV, xii, 1.
43. Ibid., IV, xii, 2.
44. Ibid., IV, xii, 3.
45. Ibid., IV, xii, 4.

46. Ibid., IV, xii, 5.

47. He quotes Paul: "that his spirit may be saved in the Day of the Lord [1 Cor. 5:5]." Ibid., IV, xii, 5 (II, p. 1233).

48. Ibid., IV, xii, 8–13.

49. Ibid., IV, xii, 10.

50. *The Register of the Company of Pastors of Geneva in the Time of Calvin*, ed. and trans. Philip Edgcumbe Hughes (Grand Rapids, MI: Wm. B. Eerdmans, 1966), p. 41.

51. Ibid., pp. 35f.

52. Ibid., p. 7.

53. It is possible that the absence of any detailed definition or exposition of the church in the later Confessions was due to the fact that they were either consciously or unconsciously following the example of the ancient creeds. It should be noted that there was no authoritative statement on the church in Western Catholicism until Vatican II.

54. 400th Anniversary Edition, tr. Allen O. Miller and M. Eugene Osterhaven (New York: United Church Press, 1963), pp. 54–56; Philip Schaff, ed., *The Creeds of Christendom* (1877, etc.), III, 307–55.

55. *The Book of Confessions, UPUSA*, 3.18. Schaff, op. cit., pp. 437ff.

56. Ibid.

57. *The Book of Confessions, UPUSA*, 3.25.

58. Ibid., 5.001–260. Cf. Schaff, op. cit., pp. 233–306, 831–909. Chapter XVII is *The Book of Confessions, UPUSA*, 5.124–41.

59. Ibid., 5.142–68.

60. Ibid., 5.133.

61. Ibid., 5.134–35.

62. Ibid., 5.137.

63. Ibid., 5.141.

64. Ibid., 5.131.

65. Ibid., 6.001–178. I have dealt with the "Grand Debate" between Presbyterians and Congregationalists in the Westminster Assembly in more detail in *The Assembly of the Lord*.

66. Cf. the Preface to the Cambridge Platform of 1648, Williston Walker, *The Creeds and Platforms of Congregationalism* [1893] (New York: The Pilgrim Press, 1960), pp. 194ff.

67. *The Book of Confessions, UPUSA*, 6.125–30, 6.131–33, 6.154–57, 6.158–61.

68. Cf. the Preface to the Cambridge Platform of 1648, Walker, ed., *Creeds and Platforms*, op. cit., pp. 194–95.

69. E.g., William Apollonius, and the Dutch classis of Walcheren, although apparently they did not manage to convince Gisbert Voet, "the pope of Utrecht."

70. Cf. *The Assembly of the Lord*, op. cit., pp. 6ff.

71. Perry Miller, *Orthodoxy in Massachusetts* (Cambridge, MA: Harvard University Press, 1933), pp. 58, 64.

72. In *A Disswasive from the Errours of our Time* (1646).

73. *An Apologeticall Narration*, p. 3.

74. Ibid., p. 10.

75. Ibid.

76. Ibid., p. 11.

77. B.H. Streeter, *The Primitive Church* (London and New York: Macmillan, 1929), p. ix.

78. From Edward Winslowe's *Hypocrisie Unmasked* (1646). It was a defense of the governor and company of Massachusetts against the slanders of Samuel Gorton of Rhode Island. Reprinted by Burt Franklin (New York, n.d.), pp. 97–98.

79. Ernst Troeltsch, *Die Soziallehren der Christlichen Kirchen und Gruppen*, Trans. Olive Wyon, *The Social Teaching of the Christian Churches* (New York: Macmillan, 1931).

80. Cf. Robert S. Paul, *The Church in Search of Its Self* (Grand Rapids, MI: Wm. B. Eerdmans, 1972), pp. 18ff., 39ff.

81. Troeltsch, op. cit., I:336.

Chapter 4   Assessment of Traditional Ecclesiologies

1. Cf. the seventeenth-century writer Katherine Chidley.

2. In a conversation on a train going out of Amsterdam in 1948. It was a statement I had ample opportunity of proving during my service at the Ecumenical Institute (WCC), Château De Bossey, Switzerland.

3. One is reminded of the words penned by John Stokesly, Bishop of London, when he was asked by Cranmer to translate the book of Acts for a vernacular version of the Bible: "I marvel at what my lord of Canterbury meaneth, that thus abuseth the people, in giving them liberty to read the Scriptures, which doth nothing but infect them with heresy. I have never bestowed an hour on my portion, nor never will. And therefore my lord shall have his book again, for I will never be guilty of bringing the simple people into error." Strype, *Cranmer*, I:71.

4. Peter Taylor Forsyth, "Authority and Theology," *The Hibbert Journal*, vol. 4 (October), 1905.

5. Peter Taylor Forsyth, *Positive Preaching and the Modern Mind* (New York: Armstrong, 1908), p. 41. Cf. the reprint edition *P.T. Forsyth, the Man, the Preacher's Theologian, Prophet for the 20th Century: A Contemporary Assessment* by Donald G. Miller, Browne Barr, and Robert S. Paul (Pittsburgh: Pickwick Press, 1981).

Chapter 5   The Old and the New

1. 1976 edition of the UCC Constitution and Bylaws, #1.

2. Ibid., #2.

3. Ibid.

4. Ibid.

5. Ibid., #3.

6. Cf. "COCU and Covenant," *Austin Seminary Bulletin*, vol. 96, Special Issue, March 1981.

7. Cf. Robert S. Paul, *The Church in Search of Its Self* (Grand Rapids, MI: Wm. B. Eerdmans, 1972), pp. 120–62, 357f. See also *infra*, chapter 9.

Chapter 6   The Doctrine of the Church (I)

1. Cf. Matthew 10:26–28; John 14:10–12, 15–17; 15:26–27; 16:12–15.

2. We have to take this point with great seriousness because repeatedly, in the history of the church, groups have arisen because of the inability of the church to carry the gospel effectively, and then, when rejected by the "mainline" churches, they have themselves been pushed into sectarianism. We have to ask ourselves seriously how far the inflexibility of the church itself causes sectarianism.

3. The healing of the deaf man with the impediment (Mark 7:36), the healing of the leper (Matthew 8:4; Luke 5:14), and the healing of Jairus' daughter (Luke 8:56).

4. Robert S. Paul, *The Church in Search of Its Self* (Grand Rapids, MI: Wm. B. Eerdmans, 1972), pp. 301–2.

5. Reported in *The Hartford Courant*.

6. Cf. Cynthia M. Campbell, "Imago Trinitatis: On the Being of God as the Model for Ministry," *Austin Seminary Bulletin* (Faculty Ed.), vol. 102, no. 4 (October 1986).

7. P.T. Forsyth, *The Principle of Authority* (1913; London: Independent Press, 1952), p. 60.

Chapter 7   The Doctrine of the Church (II)

1. William L. Langer, *The Diplomacy of Imperialism, 1890–1902* (New York: Alfred A. Knopf, 1935, 2 vols.), I:85 (cf. pp. 85–99).

2. Cf. W. Braatz et al., *Manners, Morals, Movement* (Berkeley: University of California, 1970), II:168.

3. As translated by Edward Caswall; quoted in *The Atonement and the Sacraments* (Nashville: Abingdon Press, 1960), p. 379.

4. Cf. Paul Crow, "COCU and Covenant," *Austin Seminary Bulletin,* March 1981.

5. Ibid., p. 60.

6. Ibid., p. 21.

7. John Baillie, *Invitation to Pilgrimage* (London: Oxford University Press, 1942).

8. Cf. *supra* p. 7.

9. Crow, "COCU and Covenant," op. cit., p. 44.

10. Eugene March, "Because the *Lord* Is Lord: Old Testament Covenant Imagery and Ecumenical Commitment," in "COCU and Covenant," op. cit., p. 22.

11. Cf. "Polity and Practice," *New Conversations*, Fall 1979.

12. *Reliquiae Baxterianae* (London, 1696), II, i, 143.

13. Ibid., I, i, 112.

Chapter 8   The Doctrine of the Church (III)

1. Sir Thomas Browne *Religio Medici* (1642, 1643) ed. Jean-Jacques De-nonain (London: Oxford University Press, 1954), pp. 6–8 (I, ##2,3).

2. "Polity and Practice," *New Conversations*, Fall 1979, p. 22.

3. Ibid.

Chapter 9   The Place of Pragmatism

1. French translation, 1639; English translation, 1937! He was English ambassador to France, and acquainted with Descartes.

2. Robert S. Paul, *The Church in Search of Its Self* (Grand Rapids, MI: Wm. B. Eerdmans, 1972), p. 51.

3. Ibid., pp. 51f. A.R. Vidler, ed., *Soundings: Essays in Christian Understanding* (Cambridge: Cambridge University Press, 1963), p. 145.

4. Cf. the passage cited from Calvin, *supra* pp. 39f., *Institutes*, IV, x, 30.

5. Paul, *The Church in Search of Its Self*, op. cit., pp. 276f. Some italics added. See also *supra* p. 99.

6. Gibson Winter, *The Suburban Captivity of the Church* (Garden City, NY: Doubleday, 1961) Cf. Fred D. Wentzel, *Epistle to White Christians* (Philadelphia: The Christian Education Press, 1948).

7. Paul, *The Church in Search of Its Self*, op. cit., pp. 194f.

8. Winter, op. cit., p. 127.

9. Ibid.

10. Paul, *The Church in Search of Its Self*, op. cit., chapter 5.

11. Cf. Richard P. McBrien, *Do We Need the Church?* (New York: Harper & Row, 1969).

12. Cf. A. Pannekoek, *A History of Astronomy* (New York: Interscience Publishers, 1961), p. 101; Willy Ley, *Watchers of the Skies* (New York: Viking Press, 1963), pp. 28–34.

13. George A. Lindbeck, *The Nature of Doctrine: Religion and Theology in a Postliberal Age* (Philadelphia: Westminster Press, 1984), p. 7.

14. Ibid., p. 39.

Chapter 10   The Doctrine of the Church (IV): Two Ecclesiologies

1. Cf. J.C. Hoekendijk, *The Church Inside Out* (Philadelphia: Westminster Press, 1966), p. 43.

2. Peter Taylor Forsyth, *Positive Preaching and the Modern Mind* (New York: Armstrong, 1908), p. 23.

3. But actually Jesus did not make any such claims. On the contrary, he seems to have discouraged the disciples and any others who might be tempted to make claims of this kind on his behalf. Cf. Matthew 19:16ff.

4. Richard P. McBrien, *Do We Need the Church?* (New York: Harper & Row, 1969).

5. Ibid., p. 120.

6. One of the most interesting recent attempts to recast theology in contextual terms to arise among American theologians may be found in George A. Lindbeck, *The Nature of Doctrine: Religion and Theology in a Postliberal Age* (Philadelphia: Westminster Press, 1984). Cf. also *supra* pp. 191f.

7. Cf. Jack Martin Maxwell, *Worship and Reformed Theology: The Liturgical Lessons of Mercersburg* (Pittsburgh: Pickwick Press, 1976); also B.A. Gerrish, *Tradition and the Modern World* (Chicago: University of Chicago Press, 1978), chapter 2.

8. J.H. Nichols, ed., *The Mercersburg Theology* (London and New York: Oxford University Press, 1966), pp. 10f.

9. Ibid., p. 6.

10. Gerrish, *Tradition and the Modern World*, op. cit., p. 54.

11. Cf. *The Anxious Bench* in *Catholic and Reformed: Selected Theological Writings of John Williamson Nevin*, ed. Charles Yrigoyen Jr. and George H. Bricker (Pittsburgh: Pickwick Press, 1978), pp. 121–26.

12. I cannot make this quite as absolute as many followers of the "Catholic" movements would like, for I cannot help remembering that a distinction must sometimes be made between the Faith for which the church at its best has been prepared to suffer and die, and the "faith" for which the church at its worst has been prepared to torture and burn other people. There are occasions when the prophet has to stand against the discipline of the historic church, as the lives of Luther and the Reformers show us; there are times in church history when a group of Christians has to stand up for the gospel, and even be prepared to be counted sectarian. The faults of which the Mercersburg theologians charged the Puritans, and of which the Tractarians charged the Evangelicals, were themselves the reaction of Christians who were trying to revive the dead formalism of "established" churches. In that reaction the movement went too far in the opposite direction and ignored the sense of corporate responsibility that had been so strong in the established churches. Nevin and Schaff were right in their concern to bring this back to churches in America.

13. J.W. Nevin, in his sermon on the church based on Ephesians 1:23, *The Mercersburg Theology*, pp. 58f.

14. Ibid., p. 66.

15. Ibid., p. 69.

16. Ibid.

17. Ibid.

18. Ibid., p. 67.

19. Ibid.

20. J.W. Nevin, *The Anxious Bench* (2nd ed., 1844; Chambersburg, PA), pp. 128f. Cf. *Catholic and Reformed*, op. cit., p. 111.

21. Nichols, *The Mercersburg Theology*, op. cit., pp. 70f.

22. Ibid., p. 138.

23. Ibid., p. 139.

24. Ibid., p. 141.

25. Ibid., p. 71.

26. Ibid.

27. Ibid., p. 73.

28. J.W. Nevin, "Wilberforce on the Incarnation," *Mercersburg Review*, vol. 2 (1850), 196; *The Mercersburg Theology*, op. cit., p. 90.

29. Ibid., p. 80.

30. Ibid., p. 78.

31. Cf. Robert S. Paul, *The Atonement and the Sacraments* (New York: Abingdon Press, 1960), pp. 292ff., 371ff.

32. P.T. Forsyth, *The Justification of God* (London: Duckworth & Co., 1916), pp. 22f.

33. Forsyth, *Positive Preaching and the Modern Mind*, op. cit., pp. 281ff.

34. Ibid., pp. 286–87.

35. Sydney Cave, "Dr. P.T. Forsyth, the Man and His Writings," *Congregational Quarterly*, vol. 26, no. 2 (April 1948), p. 110.

36. Ibid.

37. He later took up this theme more fully in *The Principle of Authority* (1913; 2d ed., London: Independent Press, 1952).

38. Peter Taylor Forsyth, *The Person and Place of Jesus Christ* (London: Hodder & Stoughton, 1909; 6th ed., London: Independent Press, 1948).

39. Peter Taylor Forsyth, *The Work of Christ* (London: Hodder & Stoughton, 1910; 2d ed., London: Independent Press, 1938; reprint, London: Collins, 1965).

40. Peter Taylor Forsyth, *The Church and the Sacraments* (London: Longmans Green, 1917; 3d ed., London: Independent Press, 1949).

41. Ibid., p. xv.

42. Forsyth, *Positive Preaching and the Modern Mind*, op. cit., p. 105.

43. Forsyth, *The Church and the Sacraments*, op. cit., p. 12.

44. Ibid., p. 13.

45. Forsyth, *Positive Preaching and the Modern Mind*, op. cit., p. 94.

46. "Reunion and Recognition" (1917), in *Congregationalism and Reunion* (London: Independent Press, 1952).

47. Forsyth, *The Church and the Sacraments*, op. cit., pp. 80f.

48. Cf. Bryan D. Spinks, *Freedom or Order* (Allison Park, PA: Pickwick Press, 1984). This is a detailed treatment of the Eucharist in the English Congregational churches, 1550–1974.

49. Forsyth, *The Church and the Sacraments*, op. cit., pp. 81f.

50. Ibid., p. 83.

51. Cf. Paul, *The Atonement and the Sacraments*, op. cit., pp. 284f.

52. Forsyth, *The Church and the Sacraments*, op. cit., p. 140.

53. Ibid., p. 130.

54. Ibid., p. 131.

55. Ibid., p. 132.

56. Ibid., p. 16.

57. Ibid., pp. 132f.

58. Ibid., p. 133.

59. Ibid., pp. 228f.

60. Ibid., p. 238.

61. Ibid., p. 141.

62. Ibid., p. 187.

63. J.K. Mozley quoting Forsyth, ibid., p. xii.

64. Ibid., pp. 296–97; cf. pp. 237ff., 274.

Epilogue

1. Robert S. Paul, *The Church in Search of Its Self* (Grand Rapids, MI: Wm. B. Eerdmans, 1972), p. 314.

Appendix

1. "Towards an Understanding of Local Autonomy," Theological Commission of the UCC, p. 1.

2. As adopted by the General Synod, June 16, 1936, put into effect June 20, 1940, and as amended through July 1947.

3. "Towards an Understanding of Local Autonomy," op. cit., p. 1.

4. Note in Jacob's *Reasons* (quoted *supra* p. 31) the plural form "Churches" = parishes, since each parish was regarded as a "church," i.e., *ecclesia prima*.

5. As quoted *supra* p. 31 from *Reasons taken out of God's Word and the best humane testimonies proving a necessitie of reforming our Churches in England*, London, 1604, A1 verso.

6. Champlin Burrage, Perry Miller, Douglas Horton. Cf. also John von Rohr's article on Jacob, "*Extra ecclesiam nulla salus*: An Early Congregational Version," in *Church History*, vol. 36, no. 2 (June 1967), and my own article, "Henry Jacob and Seventeenth-Century Puritanism," in *Hartford Quarterly*, vol. 7, no. 3 (Spring 1967).

7. I.e., by those who organized their churches outside the Church of England and by some Puritans who remained within the Church of England parish structure with the hope of reforming it from within.

8. At the time of the merger between the E & R and CC Churches, the General Council of the CC Churches needed some leverage against the rampant independency of those who appealed to local autonomy to block the merger. When Verne Morey wrote an article that seemed to prove that Plymouth Plantation had been no more Separatist than Massachusetts Bay, this was hailed somewhat overenthusiastically by Douglas Horton, who declared: "This important monograph might have been entitled, 'Goodbye, Mr. Browne,' for it definitely and finally bows Robert Browne (the Separatist) out of Congregationalism." Cf. his introduction to Verne Morey's "History Corrects Itself," *Bulletin of the American Congregational Association*, vol. 5, no. 2 (January 1954), p. 8. Douglas Horton's own book, *Congregationalism, A Study in Church Polity*, 1952, emphasized the same Puritan non-Separatist churchmanship as the only true and definitive Congregationalism. For the reasons that prevent me from accepting the Morey thesis in toto, see my edition of *An Apologeticall Narration* (Philadelphia and Boston: United Church Press, 1963), pp. 64f., n. 18, and my article on Jacob listed in n. 6 above.

9. Quoted *supra* p. 7. The spelling will help to remind us that Browne was writing in the sixteenth century! *A Booke which sheweth the Life and Manners of all True Christians* (1582), section 35; *The Writings of Robert Browne and Robert Harrison*, ed. Albert Peel and Leland A. Carlson (London: George Allen and Unwin, 1953), p. 253.

10. Ibid., section 51, p. 270.

11. Ibid., section 51, p. 271. My italics.

12. From Thomas Hooker's *A Survey of the Summe of Church-Discipline*, extracted in Walker, *The Creeds and Platforms of Congregationalism* (Boston: Pilgrim Press, 1960), pp. 144–47.

13. Quoted from A.H. Quint on "Councils" in the *Congregational Year Book, 1859*, in Gaius Glenn Atkins and Frederick Fagley, *History of American Congregationalism* (Boston and Chicago: The Pilgrim Press, 1952), pp. 185f.

14. *"That* proud and insolent title of *Independencie* was affixed unto us, as our claime; the very sound of which conveys to all mens apprehensions the challenge of an exemption of all Churches from all subjection and dependance, or rather a trumpet of defiance against what ever *Power, Spiritual* or *Civill*; which we doe abhor and detest. . ." *An Apologeticall Narration* [1643/4], (1963), p. 23. John Cotton likewise complained: "Nor is Independency a fit name of the way of our Churches. For in some respects it is too strait, in that it confineth us within our selves, and holdeth us forth as Independent from all others." John Cotton, *The Way of the Congregational Churches Cleared (1648), p. 11*.

15. *Orthodoxy in Massachusetts* (Cambridge, MA: Harvard University Press, 1933).

16. Ibid., p. 173.

17. Ibid., p. 174, quoting Jacob's *The Divine Beginning.*

18. Ibid., p. 183, from Weld's *An Answer to W.R.*

19. Cf. the "Foreword from New England," in John Norton, *The Answer,* trans. Douglas Horton (Boston: Belknap Press, 1958), p. 15.

20. I tried to indicate this ecumenical significance in *Ministry* (Grand Rapids, MI: Wm. B. Eerdmans, 1965), pp. 177ff.

21. Perry Miller did not understand this principle. He says: "Hooker defended this sort of 'separation or rejection' as being quite different from 'excommunication,' but he was speaking somewhat equivocably, for if the procedure did not deliver over the congregation to Satan, it gave them to something which, for the time being, was worse—to social ostracism and isolation." (Op. cit., p. 192.) But with due respect to Dr. Miller, this is anachronistic nonsense. If one truly believed what seventeenth-century Puritans believed about heaven and hell, excommunication was much worse. In the communities where the churches existed—already isolated by geography—a small congregation *could* live well enough without feeling too bad about being cut off from fellowship with churches in other towns. But to be solemnly delivered over to Satan, that was something else. Furthermore, are we to infer from Miller that no social ostracism was associated with being excommunicated?

22. I use the term self-governing simply because this is the way the twentieth century sees their polity. They would have insisted that their congregations were theocratic, i.e., under the direct government of the Holy Spirit, as each member tried to understand Christ's will for the church at that time.

23. *Orthodoxy in Massachusetts*, op. cit., p. 58.

24. A parallel growth was also taking place in Britain's prestige and economy, and after the Great Reform Act of 1833, English Nonconformists were rising to unprecedented influence in national affairs. The same kind of shift took place in the way in which English Congregationalists began to align their church relations with the politics of the Victorian Liberal Party.

25. Walker, *Creeds and Platforms*, op. cit., p. 408. Article XXX of the "Platform of Polity."

26. Ibid., p. 563. The clause underlined was added at the request of Prof. Noah Porter of Yale University.

27. They can be seen in the invitation sent out for the Boston Council of 1865, and in the supporting letter addressed to the state conference by Boston ministers. Atkins and Fagley, *History of American Congregationalism*, op. cit., p. 201; *Creeds and Platforms*, op. cit., pp. 553ff.

28. Quoted in Atkins and Fagley, op. cit., p. 211. The relevant clause is italicized.